OPTIMIZE IT

10 ways to optimize your
business, your website, and
YOU

Alex Hudson

Table of Contents

Chapter 1: What does optimization mean?

What does the word "Optimization" or "Website Optimization" mean to you? Most of us think we know it but maybe, we don't really fully understand it. You may have come across several articles, e-books, blogs and even discussion forums regarding optimization on how to use it for your business.

In a published article "Google Tries To Redefine Optimization", an author questioned whether the tool called "Website Optimizer" can really help make websites naturally position well in Google and not a tool for doing multivariate or A/B testing.

According to Merriam Webster dictionary Optimization is an *act, process, or methodology of making something (as a design, system, or decision) as fully perfect, functional, or effective as possible; specifically : the mathematical procedures (as finding the maximum of a function) involved in this.*

So in terms of website it translates into an act or process or methodology of making a website as fully perfect, functional or effective as possible. Website optimization is a continuous process of improving a site to achieve business goals while delivering a great user experience. Web Site Optimization include:

1. Serving websites faster and uptime of the site

2. Search engine optimization (SEO)

3. Campaign optimization (media optimization, A/B testing, multivariate testing)

4. Landing page optimization (A/B testing, multivariate testing)

5. Conversion rate optimization (A/B testing, multivariate testing)

6. Website design

7. Usability

As you can see all the above aspects are managed by different people (or organizations). Depending on who you ask you will get a different definition of Website Optimization. Their role in the organization influences how they think about optimization which results in different definitions. All the people are correct in their definition however each definition alone is too narrow.

The people responsible for different pieces of website optimization do not understand the complete picture and are locked in their own definition of website optimization. It is now more obvious on why Website Optimizer can be confusing to a lot of people since it covers only one aspect of website optimization.

As a web analyst you should be aware of (and involved in) all the aspects of website optimization and only then you can develop a continuous process to improve the site. By being involved does not mean you have to actually do it but you have to make sure the web analytics data is driving the decisions.

It should also be your responsibility to educate all stakeholders about how best to optimize the site based on the data. You have to act as glue, connecting different aspects of optimization. [1]

Sounds difficult, right? But it's actually easy to understand but we'll need a broader way to explain it. Website Optimization is basically reviewing the design, content, navigation and layout of your website to ensure that it is achieving the best possible goal conversion rate (find out what a goal is).

We do this by firstly looking through your site and making changes that our experience has shown us makes a difference. The obvious example of this is ensuring that we have clear Call to Actions telling the visitor exactly what we want them to do on our website.

Once we have completed all the obvious improvements, we then start creating alternate landing pages (different content, headings, call to actions, pictures etc.) and split test them. So rather than relying on our opinion (which can be fallible), we know exactly what page visitors actually prefer.

Should you bother with Website Optimization?

Definitely yes! Why waste your time and money getting your website on the front page of Google and chasing traffic to your site if the majority then either bounce straight off or don't convert? We would argue that this needs to be worked on in conjunction with your Search Engine Optimisation (SEO) and Search Engine Marketing (SEM) Strategies (definition from Webanalysis.blogspot.com "what does website optimization mean")

Chapter 2: How to optimize your business

It's important to know and remember that optimization can ultimately make or not make your business.

Businesses around the world whether local or international business, small or large companies, and even online businesses or not should fully exploit website optimization since it can help your business to grow which is everybody's goal for success.

But what does it mean to optimize your business in the real world (not just your website which we'll talk about later)?

Optimizing your business in real world is the same (in intention and process) with website optimization but can be quite difficult and also frustrating.

Business optimization in the real world can be simply put as getting your name – business name – out there. This is commonly known as traditional marketing.

Traditional marketing is a rather broad category that incorporates many forms of advertising and marketing. It's the most recognizable types of marketing, encompassing the advertisements that we see and hear every day. Most traditional marketing strategies fall under one of four categories: print, broadcast, direct mail, and telephone.

Traditional Marketing Categories

- Print: Includes advertisements in newspapers, newsletters, magazines, brochures, and other printed material for distribution

- Broadcast: Includes radio and television commercials, as well as specialized forms like on-screen movie theater advertising

- Direct mail: Includes fliers, postcards, brochures, letters, catalogs, and other material that is printed and mailed directly to consumers

- Telemarketing: Includes requested calling and cold calling of consumers over the phone

Who employs Traditional Marketing?

Because it encompasses so many different strategies, nearly every company selling a product or service uses one or more types of traditional marketing as part of an overall advertising strategy. For the most part, this form of advertising depends on the company's available marketing budget.

New Forms of Marketing

While many businesses use traditional marketing methods to attract new business and clients, others have added or completely replaced traditional marketing with new or innovative marketing tactics. These fresh methods often revolve around the Internet; companies use social media tools and online ad campaigns to expand their audience (website optimization). Companies can develop webpages or blogs that provide up-to-date information on their products or services. Customers can then subscribe to news feeds and receive alerts to sales or company events. Companies with an online presence can also advertise their business on other popular websites to direct unique visitors to their company's webpage.

Advantages and Disadvantages of Traditional Marketing

While newer marketing methods do work and can increase a company's client base, completely replacing traditional marketing with the latest marketing techniques can prove dangerous. Traditional methods have a high success rate and are proven. Internet methods are subject to clients or customers having access to an online medium and being Internet savvy. With traditional marketing, anyone with a newspaper, mail service, television or radio can learn of your business or service. Rather than customers going online to find your business or service (and possibly stumbling on your competitor's website), you bring your business or service to potential customers with print advertisements and other traditional methods.

Considerations

Incorporating innovative marketing methods is an effective way to supplement your current marketing campaign. For example, you can have a print, radio or commercial spot advertising your product or service. With these advertisements, you can then plug your company's blog or social media feed. Supplementary marketing methods are great for interacting with your customers, offering special promotions and increasing your online presence. (Adapted from Smallbusiness, "Advantages, disadvantages of traditional marketing")

So what now? Adapt! Adapt the new marketing strategies both traditional and new strategies to optimize your business. Earn and influence at the same time! Organizations must constantly adapt to rapidly changing business requirements and increasing cost pressure.

Optimizing your business processes with few traditional optimization can help you allocate scarce resources more efficiently. Like what Henry Ford said, *"Coming together is a beginning; keeping together is progress; working together is success."*

Chapter 3: Don't Invest in problems, invest in solutions

Don't find fault, find a remedy.

— Henry Ford

Wise words that we really should follow and sometimes, solutions are available to us but rather, we invest to more problems. PROBLEMS! It occurs quite too often than we are comfortable. The more you invest on problems (which secretly disguises as solutions) the worse it becomes.

The question is how we get problems disguised as solutions. It's because we tend to choose the easier way rather than work hard on it (or outsmart the problem). Then we end up with more problems than solutions. A good example of this is "Social Media Overload". Social Media Overload is simply having too many social media accounts or outlets that you are not actually *engaging* anyone at all contrast to the word *social*.

This is a common problem for many small businesses and entrepreneurs; they think that having all social media websites is good but it's actually dangerous. You're spreading your business too thin and not engaging anyone at all. You can't have a solid presence thus your business plummets down. The solution: simply choose the better media – one that works well with your business or services, engage, create presence and monetize!

See what happened? Most businesses think that having all social media outlets can help their business flourish. Some will even invest to social media experts to assist them and continue to have more media outlets than they need, this results in "not-targeting" your desired audience and not getting what you need.

You might think that investing to a new technique or outlet can help you but rather becomes your problem if you don't know how to utilize it. Invest on solutions, work on it and maximize it for your success. Don't invest to problems; fads and the latest techniques and strategies might not be your "best-next step" to success.

Investing in solutions rather than problems can help your business flourish. Choose carefully and find out what you really need.

In a blog post by Marty Zwilling in Business Insider "Nine Steps to Effective Business Problem Solving", he listed great ways on how to solve problems within problems.

1. Take the time to define the problem clearly. Many executives like to jump into solution mode immediately, even before they understand the issue. In some cases, a small problem can become a big one with inappropriate actions. In all cases, real clarity will expedite the path ahead.

2. Pursue alternate paths on "facts of life" and opportunities. Remember, there are some things that you can do nothing about. They're not problems; they are merely facts of life. Often, what appears to be a problem is actually an opportunity in disguise.

3. Challenge the definition from all angles. Beware of any problem for which there is only one definition. The more ways you can define a problem, the more likely it is that you will find the best solution. For example, "sales are too low" may mean strong competitors, ineffective advertising, or a poor sales process.

4. Iteratively question the cause of the problem. This is all about finding the root cause, rather than treating a symptom. If you don't get to the root, the problem will likely recur, perhaps with different symptoms. Don't waste time re-solving the same problem.

5. Identify multiple possible solutions. The more possible solutions you develop, the more likely you will come up with the right one. The quality of the solution seems to be in direct proportion to the quantity of solutions considered in problem solving.

6. Prioritize potential solutions. An acceptable solution, doable now, is usually superior to an excellent solution with higher complexity, longer timeframe, and higher cost. There is a rule that says that

every large problem was once a small problem that could have been solved easily at that time.

7. Make a decision. Select a solution, any solution, and then decide on a course of action. The longer you put off deciding on what to do, the higher the cost, and the larger the impact. Your objective should be to deal with 80% of all problems immediately. At the very least, set a specific deadline for making a decision and stick to it.

8. Assign responsibility. Who exactly is going to carry out the solution or the different elements of the solution? Otherwise nothing will happen, and you have no recourse but to implement all solutions yourself.

9. Set a measure for the solution. Otherwise you will have no way of knowing when and whether the problem was solved. Problem solutions in a complex system often have unintended side effects which can be worse than the original problem.

People who are good at problem solving are some of the most valuable and respected people in every area. In fact, success if often defined as "the ability to solve problems." In many cultures, this is called "street smarts," and it's valued even more than "book smarts." The best entrepreneurs have both.

Chapter 4: Work smart, Not hard

What does it mean to work hard and play smart in our world now? No, it's not outsmarting the people around you and not working hard at all. Working smart and not hard means that you use all your resources fully understand it and utilize it for your success. Rather than, working hard without a concrete strategy is also working too hard. Plan ahead and you are working smart. In a great article by FYI Print Art Work Smart, Not Hard, it tells of some ways of how to do this, let's learn more.

In today's fast-paced, constantly-connected, immediate-response-expected world, it can be difficult to manage all the necessary daily tasks of your small business. It seems a never ending cycle of attracting new customers and providing service to them. The problem is when you're busy... how do you put time back in your day to attract new clients or keep your current clients engaged and coming back?

It's exhausting!

If you're like most small business owners, your resources are also limited. You lack manpower, time, and, yup, money. Mostly, you're going it alone and using an antiquated, manual, and time-consuming process with little success. "I have a jar filled with slips of paper and business cards of my customers yet I don't know what they like, what they buy, or how to connect with them." Sound familiar?

Now it's time to learn how to work smart, not hard which is actually easier said than done but you need patience to do this.

Marketing Management

Communication is necessary to keep current customers engaged and returning, as well as, attracting new customers and growing your audience and business.

Templates:

Much of your communication can be organized in templates – email blasts, automated responses to landing pages, website inquiries, and emails. Your print can be in a template too for items such as postcards/direct mail, coupons, flyers, store signage, business cards, office collateral, and etc.

Scheduling/Distribution:

Creating automated campaigns that work on "if/then scenarios" can trigger emails and direct mail to help customers stay engaged with your business. Triggers can be set after a customer's interest has been piqued, a purchase has been made, and a milestone or life event has been reached. A special offer, email, or printed card can add that personal and thoughtful touch to your business communications. Social media can be difficult to manage but automated messaging can be easily set up to automatically distribute on various networks at the right times and days for your audience.

CRM:

Most marketing automation programs offer a CRM (Customer Relationship Management) component. This component allows you to host all of your consumer data in one place, as well as, track their buying behaviors and response to marketing.

Brand Management

Inventory:

Keep track of your stock, where it's located, and when to reorder. Alerts can be set to remind you when an item is beginning to run low so that you can replenish and not fear losing a sale due to out-of-stock merchandise.

Print:

This can also be used to manage all of your marketing materials, especially pieces that are reprinted frequently. A quick click to reorder for existing material, or copy changes to an existing template, allows you to keep your brand elements locked down, while keeping materials current.

Shipment:

If you're managing multiple locations, distribution can get tricky. Brand management systems can enable you to manage inventory in multiple locations and gives specific users the ability to place orders when needed.

Reporting:

Leave behind those sliced spreadsheets and analyze all of your stock in one place. Clearly see which products or marketing is achieving the most success.

At the end of day, you can save yourself hours of tireless work.

Chapter 5: The law of reciprocity

According to the Merriam Webster Dictionary; Reciprocity is a situation or relationship in which two people or groups agree to do something similar for each other, to allow each other to have the same rights, etc.: a reciprocal arrangement or relationship.

In business, whether online or not, it applies strongly and very differently. For professionals, they can control your decision with your consent.

A book written by Robert Cialdini was beautifully summarized by Jeff Saxton of the Social Media Examiner in his post 6 Powerful Social Media Persuasion Techniques. He states examples on how to use these techniques properly on social media.

Let's be honest, you don't just want your voice to be added to the conversation; you want your voice to be heard, repeated, and valued—and your message to be influential. Ultimately, you're after influence.

So what better way to understand social media than by looking at the fundamental principles of influence as taught by Dr. Robert Cialdini, professor of psychology and marketing at Arizona State University? In his seminal book, Influence, Cialdini covers six "weapons of influence" that are hardwired into our social and cognitive minds. In other words, we can't help but behave in accordance with these laws of social interaction.

Does this sound like something useful to keep in mind during your social media engagements? Well, let's take a look six powerful persuasion techniques:

1. Reciprocation

INFLUENCE

In Cialdini's words, the rule for reciprocation *"says that we should try to repay, in kind, what another person has provided us. If a woman does us a favor, we should do her one in return; if a man sends us a birthday present, we should remember his birthday with a gift of our own; if a couple invites us to a party, we should be sure to invite them to one of ours."*

And so it is in social media: we're more likely to retweet someone who has already retweeted us. We link to people who have linked to us. And we tend to give a business far more trust after it has provided us with a lot of free value.

Used manipulatively, this turns into auto-follow bots that help you amass thousands of followers in a breathtakingly short time—none of whom may actually care what you have to say.

Used more positively and constructively, if you focus on initiating reciprocity by providing no-strings-attached value to those in your network, you'll ultimately wield far more influence. Not because the gift economy is a new fad in marketing, but because following the law of reciprocity is how we're wired as humans.

2. Commitment and Consistency

"Once we have made a choice or taken a stand, we will encounter personal and interpersonal pressures to behave consistently with that commitment. Those pressures will cause us to respond in ways that justify our earlier decision," said Cialdini.

Chances are you follow too many people on Twitter. And you're signed up for more RSS feeds and newsletters than you can really read. Objectively, purging your list of followers and unsubscribing would eliminate distractions and increase your social media signal-to-noise ratio.

But most people never make that purge and hardly ever unsubscribe. Part of it goes back to reciprocation, but a larger part stems from consistency: you're loath to admit that following and subscribing to those people and newsletters was a mistake.

On the positive side, how much more likely are you to comment on a blog that you've already commented on before? Especially, if you're now "signed in" to comment on the blog during future visits and if your Gravatar or Disqus headshot shows up next to the comments?

According to the principle of consistency, you'll want to remind people of their previous positive commitments through perks, public displays, an elimination of friction for increasing their commitment, etc. It works for Amazon prime, Amazon's 1-click ordering, and Amazon's reviewer system, and it will work for fostering blog comments and a blog community, too. □

3. Social Proof

One method we use to determine correct behavior is to find out what other people think is correct. We view a behavior as more correct in a given situation to the degree that we see others performing it.

Whether we admit it or not, most of us are impressed when someone has a ton of blog subscribers, Twitter followers, YouTube views, multiple blog reviews for their upcoming book, and so on.

Yes, people can game the system (auto-follows and such), which can jade our intellectual response, but our core and initial emotional reactions stay the same.

On the positive side, creating a lot of value for others can help companies and individuals gain social proof via reciprocation: writing engaging content for guest posts, offering to interview authors and subject matter experts, and so forth.

 Not only do these activities provide social proof in themselves, but they can help you gain a support network capable of "salting" your blog comments, your retweets, etc.

And when it comes to social proof, tribes matter. It's not just about what the mass of people are doing on social media that constitutes proof, it's what other like-minded people and peers are doing. So according to the principle of "social proof," you should concentrate your social media efforts on finding and building social proof within your tribe.

4. Liking

"We most prefer to say yes to people we know and like," says Cialdini. Extensions of this principle are:

Physical attractiveness creates a halo effect and typically invokes the principle of liking;

- We like people who are similar to us;

- We like people who compliment us;

- We like things that are familiar to us;

- Cooperation toward joint efforts inspires increased liking;

- An innocent association with either bad or good things will influence how people feel about us.

How does this work for social media? Well, to start with the virtual equivalent of physical attractiveness, we give extra credence to attractively designed blogs, messages contained in videos with higher production quality, and corporations' landing pages displaying a better sense of social media savvy in their overall design and layout.

Similarly, individuals involved in coordinating joint ventures for the common good are associated with—and therefore "haloed" by—those efforts, while at the same time invoking cooperation toward a joint effort, which further increases "liking." Think of Seth Godin's efforts at compiling free and thoughtful e-books and then using the compilation to raise funds for a non-profit.

As for complimenting others, what else is a retweet, a trackback, or a positive blog comment than a social compliment? And yes, those are all activities you should participate in authentically, sincerely, and liberally if you wish to leverage the principle of liking to your advantage.

5. Authority

Cialdini talks about *"The extreme willingness of adults to go to almost any lengths on the command of authority..."* In his book, he examines how authority can be conferred by (and also manufactured by) titles, clothes, and trappings.

In social media, authority is less about titles and clothes than about virtual trappings. In his (fantastic) report, "Authority Rules," Brian Clark talks about how perceived expertise can frequently differ from real expertise.

Meaning that the guy known for blogging about and offering intelligent commentary on a subject will likely have far more perceived expertise (and therefore influence as an authority) than a genuine but unknown non-blogging expert.

But perhaps the most direct measure of authority is the number of people who will buy or download a recommended resource based on little more than an authority's endorsement.

How many people would buy a copywriting book simply because Brian Clark said it's a must-read? How many people will download a free PDF on nothing more than Seth Godin's evaluation that it contains important insights?

But one thing social media has seemed to spark is a dawning understanding that authority is (or should be, at least) limited to a legitimate field of knowledge. So when a relatively famous figure like Robert Scoble states on his website Scobleizer that search engine optimization isn't important for small businesses, he's "taken to task" on it rather severely.

6. Scarcity

Apart from reciprocity, this is perhaps the most used tool in social media. When bloggers open up a class or inner circle membership or subscription service, it is never for an unlimited number of customers or for an always open/unlimited time. Smart bloggers either create or fully leverage already existing scarcity by limiting seats available, length of time to buy, etc.

Laura Roeder has rather famously made scarcity a centerpiece of a signature technique, wherein bloggers hold competitions with free services as a prize. When contestants don't win, they then value the prize more highly precisely because of the newly perceived scarcity. This makes them more likely to accept a consolation prize of getting the services at a slight discount.

Parting Recommendations

While the six principles of persuasion started out as "weapons of influence" that were used against us by "compliance professionals," I—along with Cialdini—would encourage you to practice the positive side of wielding influence. To sum up many of the recommendations from the post, here are some very positive ways to leverage the principles of influence to increase your social media success:

- Focus on creating value and initiating the reciprocity principle by gifting your social media contacts with high-value content, insights, reports, etc.

- Sincerely flatter your subscribers, friends, and commenters by responding to them and nurturing your growing community. Actively reach out to people you admire using social media and pay them the compliment of commenting on their blogs, following their tweets, linking to their content, etc.

- Commit to consistent engagement on the social media platforms you chose to use, to the point of staying away from new social media platforms that you don't have the resources to actively participate in.

- Use social proof as credibility cues where appropriate. Show off your number of subscribers next to the Subscribe button. Possibly use colleagues to "salt" your comments on important posts, build up your network by guest posting, commenting, and retweeting.

- Coordinate within your community on larger efforts for the greater good. You'll probably be psyched at what you create or accomplish, you'll do good and feel good about it, and you'll likely become associated with the effort.

- Put the extra effort in on achieving professional and inspiring design. Dress for success on your blog, website, and social media landing pages.

- When creating a contest or trying to spark immediate action, use the scarcity principle to positive effect. But be honest about it—no changing "last day for" dates, no miraculously replenishing supplies, etc

Chapter 6: How to optimize your website

If you don't know SEO and you are on the internet, then you are living under the rock for ages. But let's start with what is website optimization. Website optimization or also called search engine optimization (SEO), website optimization is a phrase that describes the procedures used to optimize – or to design from scratch – a website to rank well in search engines. Website optimization includes processes such as adding relevant keyword and phrases on the website, editing Meta tags, image tags, and optimizing other components of your website to ensure that it is accessible to a search engine and improve the overall chances that the website will be indexed by search engines.

An article posted by ReliableSoft gives us an overview on why website optimization or SEO is important. This is a great post because it also provides an overview introduction to SEO.

Why is SEO important?

In today's competitive market SEO is more important than ever. Search engines serve millions of users per day looking for answers to their questions or for solutions to their problems. If you have a web site, blog or online store, SEO can help your business grow and meet the business objectives.

Search engine optimization is essential because:

- The majority of search engine users are more likely to choose one of the top 5 suggestions in the results page. So to take advantage of this and gain visitors to your web site or customers to your on-line store you need to rank as high as possible.

- SEO is not only about search engines but good SEO practices improve the user experience and usability of a web site.

- User's trust search engines and having a presence in the top positions for the keywords the user is searching increases the web site's trust.

- SEO is also good for the social promotion of your web site. People who find your web site by searching Google or Yahoo are more likely to promote it on Facebook, Twitter, Google+ or other social media channels.

- SEO is also important for the smooth running of a big web site. Web sites with more than one author can benefit from SEO in a direct and indirect way. Their direct benefit is increase in search engine traffic and their indirect benefit is having a common framework (checklists) to use before publishing content on the site.

- SEO can put you ahead of the competition. If two web sites are selling the same thing, the search engine optimized web site is more likely to have more customers and make more sales.

An introduction to SEO for beginners

For beginners to SEO the above definition may sound complicated so in simpler terms Search Engine Optimization is a way to improve your web site so that it will appear closer to the top positions in the search results of Google, Yahoo, Bing or other search engines.

When you perform a search on Google (or any other search engine) the order by which the returning results are displayed, is based on complex algorithms. These algorithms take a number of factors into account to decide which web site (or blog) should be shown in the first place, second place etc.

Optimizing your web site for search engines will give you an advantage over non-optimized sites and you increase your chances to rank higher.

What are the main stages of the Search Engine Optimization process?

As I mentioned above, SEO is not a static process but rather a framework with rules and processes. For simplicity though SEO can be broken down into 2 main stages:

- On-site SEO: What rules to apply on your site to make it search engine friendly and

- Off-site SEO: How to promote your web site or blog so that it can rank better in search results.

On-site SEO

When we say on-site, it means simple tweaks you can do to your web site and increase your search engine visibility, such as, descriptions, tags and Meta descriptions. That simply stated, anything that you can do on your website to get better visibility. We will add 15 SEO tips provided once again by ReliableSoft.

If you seriously take into account these 2 factors i.e. web site structure and the SEO tips, then that's all you need to do to help search engines trust your web site. There is no need to spend more time than needed with on-site SEO neither you should over optimize your web site or blog because it can sometimes (under certain conditions) generate the opposite results.

Off-site SEO

Besides the changes you can do to your web site (on-site SEO) so that it ranks higher in the SERPs, the other way to improve your web site's ranking position is by using off-site SEO techniques.

Off-site SEO is generally known as link building but I prefer to use the term web site promotion since a proper way to promote a web site involves much more methods and techniques than building links.

In general, search engines are trying to find the most important pages of the web and show those first when a user enters a search query. One of the factors to determine the position a web page will appear in the results is the number of incoming links.

Incoming links are a signal of trust and depending from where the links are coming, they can greatly affect your ranking position (either positively if the links are coming from well-known and trusted sites or negatively if they are paid links, article directories, link farms etc.).

What can you do to get more links?

That's a very good question and I am sure that if you search the Internet for that phrase you will get hundreds of different answers. In my opinion, and this is what I will try to explain in this book, you should forget about building links and concentrate on creating good quality content for your web site.

Good content will get you natural links which in turn will give you good rankings and traffic. If you try to buy links or get them the easy way, you may have a temporary success and then see your web site disappearing from the top pages after the next Google update.

What is the difference of SEO and Internet marketing?

Some people often ask me "Is SEO the same as Internet Marketing?" The simplest answer I can give is that SEO is one of the tools available in your Internet Marketing arsenal. It is not Internet Marketing as such but it can be part of your overall Internet Marketing campaign which normally includes other things like social media promotion, content strategy etc.

Good content is still the most important success factor with or without SEO

Before closing this introduction to search engine optimization you must have very clear in your mind that SEO cannot help you if you don't have good content.

In other words if you try to SEO a web site with not very good content your chances of succeeding (in the long term) are minimum. On the other hand a web site with good content can do well with or without SEO. SEO will just give the web site an extra boost.

SEO is a must for every web property

To sum it up, Search engine optimization or SEO is a way to optimize your web site so that search engines will understand it better and give you higher rankings. It is important since a good SEO approach can drive more traffic to your web site, blog or on-line store and gain more customers, make sales and fulfill your business purpose.

Now let's start learning on how to optimize your website. As mentioned earlier, we will include the 15 Ways to Google boost Your Website for the On-site optimization.

As a beginner or not to SEO, you need to understand that there is no magic way to rank your web site in the first page of Google, Bing or Yahoo. Search engines are governed by complex algorithms and it takes a lot of effort to 'convince' them that your web site or page deserves one of the top spots.

Nevertheless, there are certain rules you can follow to optimize your web site and provide the bots with the necessary signals. While the web is floated with SEO tips and advice these are explained in a theoretical level and not how they can be applied in practice.

1. Page Titles and description

Page titles

Page titles are a very important aspect of SEO and this is why it is first on the list. My findings the last couple of months show that page titles are more important than ever especially for Google SEO.

For now the most important characteristics of a page title are:

- Each page needs to have a unique page title that accurately describes the page's content.

- Be brief and descriptive.

- Help the user understand what the page is about

Home page title:

The title for your homepage can list the name of your website/business and could include other bits of important information like the physical location of the business or maybe a few of its main focuses or offerings.

For example:

Calorie Secrets – Weight Loss Tips, Diet and Fitness advice for a ...
www.caloriesecrets.net/
Discover the **secrets** behind **calories** and learn how to lose weight healthy with our Weight loss tips, diet and fitness guides.Free tools and advice from experts.
How many calories should I ... - About - 50 Tips for weight loss and a ... - Contact

Post/other pages title: Title of other posts/pages of your web site should accurately describe what the page is about and be attractive for the searcher.

How many calories should I burn a day to **lose weight?**
www.caloriesecrets.net/how-many-calories-should-i-burn-a-...
 by Alex Chris - in 1,409 Google+ circles - More by Alex Chris
29 Mar 2012 – Use our calorie calculator to calculate **how many calories** you need to eat and burn per day if you want to **lose weight**. We explain the process ...

Description: A page's description Meta tag is also very important. It gives users, Google and other search engines a summary of what the page is about. Google may choose to show what you type in the description as a snippets for your page or may decide to use a part of your page's content.

In other words it does not mean that what you write in the description will show in the snippet.

The guidelines for writing a good description are:

- Always provide a unique description for all pages, post, products of your website.

- Keep the size between 150-160 characters.

- Avoid repeating the title in the description

- Don't add too many keywords

- Try to use the description as a way to 'advertise' your page to the reader so that they click on your title and visit the page.

2. Permanent link structure

The permanent link structure is a term used to describe the format of URLS for pages (categories/tags) or individual posts of a web site. It is shown in the browser address bar and in the search results (below the page title).

Guidelines for optimized link structure

- Make Urls simple and easy to understand for search engines and users

- Use hyphens ' – ' to separate the words that make up a url

- Avoid lengthy Urls with unnecessary information

- Use words that describe what the page is about but avoid keyword stuffing

Examples of BAD url structures:

- http://www.example.com/UK/123213/5005.html

- http://www.example.com/socialmedianews

- http://www.example.com/id=7&sort=A&action=70

Examples of GOOD url structures

- http://www.example.com/social-media-news

- http://www.example.com/2002/12/social-media-news

3. Breadcrumb

Make sure that you have a breadcrumb in all your internal pages. A breadcrumb is a set of links at the top of the page that aid navigation. If you are using WordPress there are many free plugins to create a breadcrumb.

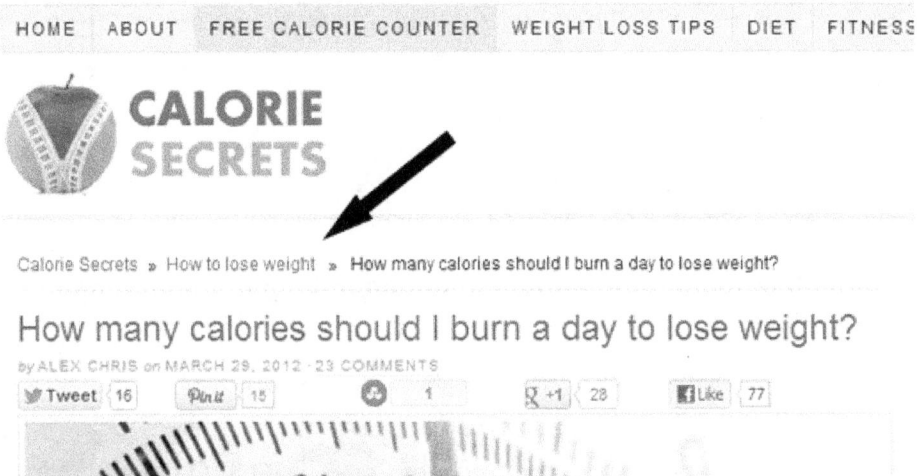

4. Internal links

When we talk about internal links we mean links in a page that point to other pages within the web site i.e. not external links. In the example below if you were to click on the link with anchor "increase the intensity" you would be redirected to a page with-in the web site to find out more information on how to increase the intensity of an exercise.

2. There are different ways in which the above exercises can be performed, so other variations can be as good and even better some times. Just always make sure you perform an exercise with the correct technique and within your fitness level.

3. Do make sure you <u>increase the intensity</u> or change your workout every few weeks in order to provide adequate and progressive overload for the muscles. You can increase the intensity by adding weights were applicable or just changing the exercise slightly. Alternatively swap the exercises and try some new ones. Keep your workouts interesting.

4. Do consult a medical professional if you do have any health complaints before taking any exercise on.

5. Very important: do warm up and cool down before you do any exercise.

Internal linking is a very important factor for web site SEO but still many web site owners are not using it correctly. The rules to follow for internal links are simple:

- Link related articles together either by using keyword anchor text or by using the full article title

- Make sure that the links are useful both for the user and easy to understand by search engines.

- Don't make links for search engines only. An internal link should help the user navigate the site better.

- Do not use terms like 'click here' or '[..]' for internal linking.

- Don't overdo it. 4-5 internal links per page are enough (create more if really necessary)

Don't always link old posts from new posts but every couple of weeks go back and link newer posts from older posts. It's not an easy task to do especially if you have a lot of posts but it's a very valuable tool for on-site SEO.

5. Text formatting and the use of H1, H2 and H3

Don't just publish text on your web site without first doing some basic formatting. This is not good for the user experience and works against your SEO efforts. General guidelines for formatting a post or page on your web site:

- Use H1 tags for the title of your post

- Use H2 tags for the main headings of your post.

- Use BOLD and Italics to draw users attention

- Don't use H2 tags for all your headings

- Write small paragraphs

- Use a font size that is easy to read

When formatting your posts always have in mind the user experience. Can the user identify the main sections of your post (H2 tags) just by looking at the page? Is the text easy to read even on other devices (Apple Ipads, Android tablets etc)?

Here is an example of a proper page formatting for articles.

Wearing the right clothes can do miracles in disguising the imperfections, but wouldn't be nice sometimes to wear whatever you like rather than what you have to? So instead of avoiding the strapless dress to hide the arms why not get fit arms. To get toned arms is probably quite easy although it does at times seem that the chicken wings never leave.

The shoulders and back don't tend to store a lot of fat so when toned they seem to show nicely. I do tend to favor functional exercises rather than static one muscle at the time jobs, so as you may expect there will be a few functional exercise solutions to add to your workout.

Can diet make your arms more muscular and firm?

Not per se but in some ways yes. It may be, that under the layer of fatty tissue there is a fine firm and well worked muscle hiding and all it needs is to be unveiled. Exercise is not the mean to all ends, and yes it will help with weight loss and __fat burning__ but diet does play a major role.

6. The 404 Page

SEO is about improving the user experience and a proper 404 page contributes to that goal. The 404 page is the page shown when a user is looking for a page on your site that doesn't exist or mistypes a URL or follows a broken link. When the 404 page is not configured it looks like this:

The page cannot be found

The page you are looking for might have been removed, had its name changed, or is temporarily unavailable.

Please try the following:

- Make sure that the Web site address displayed in the address bar of your browser is spelled and formatted correctly.
- If you reached this page by clicking a link, contact the Web site administrator to alert them that the link is incorrectly formatted.
- Click the Back button to try another link.

HTTP Error 404 - File or directory not found.
Internet Information Services (IIS)

Technical Information (for support personnel)

- Go to Microsoft Product Support Services and perform a title search for the words HTTP and 404.
- Open IIS Help, which is accessible in IIS Manager (inetmgr), and search for topics titled Web Site Setup, Common Administrative Tasks, and About Custom Error Messages.

This is not useful for the user and negatively impacts the user experience.

A properly configured 404 page should:

- Give some info to the user of what happened rather than displaying "Not found"

- Have a design consistent with the rest of the website

- Give options to the user to navigate to other pages of the site.

If you are using a professional theme (like Thesis), it takes care of the 404 page. This is a good example of what a 404 page looks like:

Calorie Secrets

You 404'd it. Gnarly, dude.

Surfin' ain't easy, and right now, you're lost at sea. But don't worry; simply pick an option from the list below, and you'll be back out riding the waves of the Internet in no time.

- Hit the "back" button on your browser. It's perfect for situations like this!
- Head on over to the home page.
- Punt.

7. Image Optimization

Images are sometimes necessary to enhance the user experience but care should be taken not to create other side effects like problems with page load speed or slow response. Especially after the success of Pinterest many webmasters started using more images in their posts. If you do decide to use images, mind the following:

- Use Alt Text to describe the image. You can add keywords but don't overdo it.

- Use keywords in image filenames (separated with dashes). Avoid using filenames like image1.jpg or person1.jpg. Instead use meaningful names with dashes. For example woman-working-out.jpg

- Keep all image files in a dedicated folder in your site i.e. www.mydomain.com/images/

- Optimize the image size. The smaller the size of the image (in KB) the faster is your web site. You can use this free tool from Yahoo to make your image size smaller without losing the quality.

8. Page Speed

Google has many times said that page speed is a ranking factor and yet many webmasters don't optimize their web sites for speed. Their aim (Google's) is to provide the searcher with the most accurate results in the fastest possible way. It is certain that page speed (as a ranking factor) will gain more importance in the next couple of years.

Fast web sites improve the user experience and it is a factor to encourage the visitor to come again. In addition, a web site that loads in less than 8 seconds is more likely to:

- Rank better in search results

- Get more page visits per user

- Get more conversions

How to tackle the page speed problem?

- Remove any unnecessary plug-ins (if you are using WordPress) or java script from the pages.

- Optimize the size of your images

- Use a caching service or plug-in (I use WP Super cache and W3Total Cache).

- Go to http://www.webpagetest.org/ and test how many seconds it takes for your pages to load from different locations, internet speed and browsers. The analysis report at the end will also tell you which components of your page take too long to load so that you can remove them.

- Go to Google Page Speed Service to analyze your web site and get performance recommendations.

- If you have a lot of images on your site and you cannot improve performance with the recommendations given by the tools mentioned above you can consider using a CDN (Content Delivery Network) service such as Cloud Flare or Amazon Cloud Front

9. Google authorship

What is Google authorship status?

It's a way to bind your content with your Google+ profile. When you do that successfully your picture appears in the Google search results next to your content.

How Google authorship status relates to Search Engine Optimization?

- It improves the credibility of a web site in both the minds of users and search engines.

- Studies have shown that more people are likely to click a link from the search results if the author is verified.

- You increase the chances of getting natural links (people are more likely to link to your web site or page if you are verified).

- There is also a confirmed hidden benefit from authorship status which gives you additional listings in the SERPS.

How to get a Google authorship status? You can follow the instructions here: https://support.google.com/webmasters/answer/6083347

10. Mobile friendly web sites

A significant number of searches performed each day are through mobile devices. Many studies over the last 6 months identified that the number of searches using smartphones is steadily increasing especially when it comes to making online purchases. It's not in the scope of this book to go in detail into mobile SEO but there are some simple steps to follow to ensure that your web site is mobile friendly.

- First thing to do is understand the difference between a mobile friendly web site and a native Android, iPhone or Windows Mobile app.

- A mobile friendly web site is optimized for viewing on the mobile browser (i.e. Chrome on android or Safari on iPhone). A native android (iPhone or Windows Mobile app) is an application that can be downloaded from the mobile markets (Google Play or Apple Store

- The easiest way to create a mobile friendly web site is to use a plugin (if you are using WordPress) or a service (there are free and paid) which will optimize your web site for mobiles.

11. User Sitemap

A sitemap is a list of all posts/pages of your web site. You need 2 types of sitemaps. First an xml sitemap to submit to Google, Bing and other search engines and second an html sitemap to help visitors find your content easier. It is recommended to place a link to your user sitemap from the main menu.

XML Sitemap (for search engines): Depending on your blogging platform you can use plugins to create and update your web site's sitemap. When viewed in the browser it looks like this:

http://www.caloriesecrets.net/how-to-get-toned-arms-for-women/

http://www.caloriesecrets.net/how-to-control-portion-sizes-when-losing-weight/

http://www.caloriesecrets.net/references/

http://www.caloriesecrets.net/is-it-bad-to-eat-carbs-at-night/

http://www.caloriesecrets.net/how-much-cardio-to-lose-weight-fast/

http://www.caloriesecrets.net/how-to-lose-belly-fat-strictly-for-women/

http://www.caloriesecrets.net/readers-qa-im-finding-it-hard-to-shed-the-last-few-pounds/

http://www.caloriesecrets.net/5-ways-to-keep-your-heart-in-good-shape/

http://www.caloriesecrets.net/does-vitamin-d-help-with-weight-loss/

http://www.caloriesecrets.net/how-to-stop-junk-food-addiction/

http://www.caloriesecrets.net/10-healthy-bedtime-snacks/

HTML Sitemap (for Users): The user sitemap should provide links to all (or to the most important pages of your site). It can also group posts by author, date, category etc. Its purpose is to help the user find information on your site easier and quicker. An example of a user sitemap looks like this:

Categories

- Diet and Nutrition Advice
- Fitness
- How to lose weight
- Weight Loss Tips

Archives

- November 2012
- October 2012
- September 2012

12. Content is still king

In order for the above tips to work you need first and foremost to have good content on your web site. Content is still king and a web site with good, original, quality content can do better in the long run (with or without SEO) than a web site optimized in SEO but with not so good content.

What is good content?

When people search on Google, Yahoo or Bing they are essentially looking for answer to a question. Good content is post or page that answers this question.

How do I know if my content is good?

There are two simple ways to understand if your content is useful. First you can check your analytics and especially the time spent on a page. A reader will stay longer on the page if the content is good and second the number of social media shares (Facebook likes, tweets etc.). This is actually a very good way to understand what user's want and what type of content to provide in your web site or blog.

How to write good content?

There is no simple answer to this question but the following guidelines can put you in the correct direction:

- Make sure that your content delivers what is promised in the title. If for example your title is "How to lose 15 pounds of fat" make sure that your post provides an accurate description (or steps) that someone can follow to achieve the desired result.

- Check your text for typos, spelling and grammar mistakes.

- Format your text

- Provide links within your content (where appropriate) to other pages on your site (or other sites) to get more information.

- Include references from established research or studies (where appropriate) to prove that what you are saying or suggesting is correct.

Quantity VS Quality

Many people often ask me "How long (in words) should I make my posts?" You should understand that there is no single answer that fits all purposes. It greatly depends on the type of post and topic.

If for example you are writing about the benefits of black chocolate then surely you won't have to write that much. This is exactly where quantity vs. quality comes into place. It's better to write a quality post without counting words rather than a long unfriendly post for the sake of providing more word count.

13. Fresh Content

Having fresh content is an incentive for visitors to come back and for search engine bots to visit and crawl your web site more often.

This is true when you really have something new to say about the niche or topic your covering. Avoid publishing pages with similar content just for the sake of updating your web site or blog.

14. Check your external links

External links (links in your web site pointing to other sites) are important for SEO. In general ensure that:

- You are not linking to spam web sites or web sites with inappropriate content

- You have no broken links i.e. links to web sites or pages that no longer exist (you can use xenu – a free tool to analyze your external links).

- You are not in any way selling or exchanging links

- Any links in your comments section carry the no-follow directive

15. Webmaster tools and Analytics

Google and Bing have what is called webmaster tools. This is the place to register and submit your web site to their index. After submission you can visit the webmaster central and get valuable information about your web site.

Although this is not directly related to SEO when you submit your web site to Google webmaster tools and Bing webmaster tools you gain a number of advantages:

- It's a way to tell search engines about your web site (by submitting your sitemap)

- It's a way to get feedback on the number of pages indexed

- It's a way to get notified about potential problems i.e. access issues that restrict web sites from crawling your content

- You can see the number of incoming and internal links.

Also, it is very important to use Google Analytics (or any other traffic analysis tool) to:

- Find out how visitors find your web site (direct visits, search, referrals etc)

- How much time they spend on your pages (and on which pages)

- What keywords they used

- How many pages they view per visit

I have followed all the above tips, now what?

Once you have optimized your web site for SEO by following ALL of the above guidelines the next steps are:

- Concentrate on improving your web site by following these 15 steps

- Promote your web site using techniques that work and above all are safe. If you fail with your SEO optimization your web site may not be running on its full potential but if you follow wrong promotion techniques you increase the risk of getting a penalty and completely destroy your efforts.

Chapter 7: The law of correspondence

Depending on what field, the word correspondence differs but for social media it focuses on "communication". According to The Business Dictionary, correspondence is any written or digital communication exchanged by two or more parties. Correspondences may come in the form of letters, emails, text messages, voicemails, notes, or postcards. Correspondences are important for most businesses because they serve as a paper trail of events from point A to point B.

This is very important and there are many things you should know and understand about correspondence. A wonderful post from Numerounonweb tackles correspondence on a daily basis. Day-to-Day Correspondence: How Even Just a Little Regular Social Media Marketing Can Help Your Online Business Over Time can explain further.

Slow and Steady

With online business success, like financial investments and real estate interactions, you can bet there is some debate on what processes work better than others. It's not yet all down pat—online business is a relatively new phenomenon, and how it can work the most effectively for a business hasn't been completely understood.

One online business area that gets a bit more scrutiny than others is social media optimization (SMO), including how to use social media for business success. A lot of critics say that it's too much work to gain real success from SMO, and others dismiss it as being fun for youngsters but not a serious business tool. To be fair, these criticisms have some truth to them—social media is not like pay-per-click (PPC) advertising or search engine optimization (SEO) in terms of gaining real wealth from online.

But social media for online business purposes does have its advantages. It might not bring success in fast, booming instances, but it can bring in some regular success slowly and steadily. Social media seems to be able to attract people over time, and while it might not be what seems like a huge success, it can be worthwhile and potentially lead to bigger success stories down the line.

It's important to reconsider social media these days. It can surprise you as to how much success it can generate—you just have to stick with it.

Regular Updates

Once you've got your business registered with specific social media web sites, it's time to get into some frequent and regular practice of keeping an updated profile. This is what can bring in gradual client interest.

Taking advantage of a social media blog is always a good idea. Regular updates and information on your blog, no matter how small, can let the public know what you're up to, how your business has developed, and what they can look out for. However, not regularly maintaining your blog can kill off interest from the public, so it's best to follow some sort of schedule for update action.

This invariably leads to offering new promotions or special products or services through your social media web sites. People love checking out social media for what's new and exciting in the world, so why don't you become part of the excitement itself? If you think of the big corporations that use social media, a lot of their specific promotions are heavily showcased on social media—and in some cases only on social media. Again, this is a good cue for you to take.

Of course, it's never good to disregard whatever social media optimization techniques are available or become available. Every time you do your updates, make sure your content is up to social media SEO standards, ready to be found through organic searches online. You should always have the best possible online business success channels open, and good social media optimization combined with regular usage can only help keep those channels wide open.

Come Again

As mentioned, using social media for online business success means maintaining it regularly; preferably on some sort of schedule. This might not seem that appealing to you, but if you want to use social media, getting some sort of social media management process incorporated into your business is necessary. Whether you do it, or another employee does, either party has to again and again revisit the social media site to input regular updates.

Some people don't think social media is serious for online business success. But the truth is that, while being fun, it has a lot potential for generating success. When you use social media for your online business, keep your duties regular, while still enjoying yourself—your clients will respond to both.

And now let's learn How to improve your social media, phone and email correspondence in this post from Bookbon by Kathrin Tschiesche.

The discipline of networking is all about identifying whom you know, nurturing the people that you know, and expanding your network with new people that you need to know. Once you have built a strong network of competent people who are exceptionally talented in areas where you are weak, you will represent a much larger area of knowledge than you would if you were on your own.

Your network is your safest bet when it comes to development of competences. You can educate yourself and take all the courses you wish, but nothing compares with a loyal competent network — it's compact, informative, and the direct path to successful individual and organizational performance. Here are some tips on how to maintain your network by choosing the right way of corresponding with your network — via email, phone or social media.

Networking correspondence

E-mails:

Many of us write e-mails to each other including after a conference. E-mails are still the most widely used method of contact. E-mails can be good, but they can also be unsuitable. People receive a lot of e-mails, and it can be difficult to remember all the e-mails that are received because they all look alike. Learn how to write good e-mails that people want to read and will remember.

Here is one example of a very typical e-mail:

Dear XXX

Thank you for the meeting on [date]. At the meeting we agreed to blah blah.

I will follow-up and will get back you as soon as possible blah blah.

Kind regards,

XXX

Have you received similar e-mails? How did it make you feel? Did you feel like meeting the sender?

What is wrong with these e-mails are the following:

- The introduction is rather impersonal. The e-mail is not relevant because it does not link the sender and receiver together. They lack something that makes the reader think "I have to take care of this, and therefore, I will read the e-mail."

- The e-mail is too short. E-mails should be short, but not too short. Take the time to be personal. TIP: Test the quality of your e-mails by adding some of your colleagues as CC so that you will get some feedback on your e-mails.

- No urgent action. The e-mails do not ask the receiver to do something urgently. He gets the impression that he is only asked to keep his eyes and ears open, and that is rather noncommittal. The same rules apply to letters. Be personal and relevant. Letters and e-mails can be written in accordance with the PRAC method: P= Personal, R= Relevant, A= Action, C= Contact.

Be personal (sometimes senders do not write a name in their e-mails; the letter just reads "Dear Customer"). Sometimes people just write a general e-mail or letter and send it to everybody in the network without addressing it to specific persons. That does not work. You will find that people will not get back to you when you write to a large group of people.

People want to feel that you are engaging with them directly and personally. If you absolutely must send mass e-mails and letters, then you must not do what everyone else does. You have to think about the people who receive your e-mail or letter and why they should read it.

Phone and text messages:

When you call people or leave a message, you show presence and initiative, and the person you are calling can sense your mood, and vice versa. E-mail is efficient but try calling the person 30% of the time. You will be surprised how much it brings to a relationship.

Leave a message if the person does not answer the phone. Make it brief, concrete, and personal. Smile while you are speaking, it will increase the probability that you will be someone people will actually call back. Your message should be less than one minute and include a request for further dialogue.

Social media:

Social media is here to stay whether you like it or not. The people that you will likely want to connect with are increasingly active on platforms such as Facebook, LinkedIn, Google+, and Twitter. Social media is useful for: information and knowledge sharing; file sharing; connecting on a professional and personal level; and for marketing, fostering loyalty, and cooperation between people.

General networking tips

- Be yourself—the best version of yourself

- Be strategic, selective, and thoughtful about who you network with (quality rather than quantity)

- Ask what and how questions to invite people to talk about what is on their mind

- Express needs clearly so that other people can understand you and help you

- Remember to say thank you when people help you so that they will want to help you again and again

- Remember to help other people if you can so that they will like you

- If you cannot help a person always offer the person an alternative

- Be someone to rely on so that people will want to share something with you

- Make your preparations before participating at events to avoid wasting your time and the company's resources

- Be good at making contact so that people feel they are in good company when they are with you

Chapter 8: How to optimize yourself

The chase for success is a constant struggle. Success is often determined by one or two opportunities that you are presented with. If you do not capitalize on those opportunities then you may not get another chance. In order to capitalize on those opportunities you must be 100% committed to being prepared for when those opportunities arise. If you really want to be successful why not put yourself in the best position possible when opportunity comes knocking.

Here are 7 Ways to Optimize Yourself For Success written by Alex Palmiere from Motivation Grid.

1. Get enough sleep

How do you feel after a night of poor sleep? I know for myself personally if I get less than 8 hours of sleep I feel like hell. I am sluggish in the morning and it takes me until at least mid-afternoon to get fully into my day. I realized that this is terrible.

What if opportunity comes knocking in the early morning and I am too drowsy to take advantage? Make sure you are getting however much sleep you need to perform at your optimum level. Only you know how much that is. Optimize yourself for success!

2. Exercise daily & Eat Healthy

If your body is not in its best possible shape, than your mind will not be performing at its highest possible level. Think about it. If you're driving a truck with a ton of weight in the back and the wrong oil in the engine, will it run to its full potential? Absolutely not. Your body is no different. Exercise daily and be sure to eat as healthy as you can. Food is the fuel you're putting into your body. If you are living off fried chicken, then your body will output those results. If you're living on a clean diet then it will output those results.

3. Carry a journal

How many times have you thought of an idea and said, "Man, that's a really great one," only to forget the idea some time later.

You never know when an idea will come to you or when inspiration will strike. Carry a small journal with you at all times so you can easily write down any ideas that come to you.

4. Maintain a schedule & maximize your time

I used to go through my day without a plan and find myself watching YouTube at around 3 every day. I didn't know how I ended up there but before I knew it hours had passed. I now keep a schedule and allow allotted times for amusement so I don't get sidetracked.

If you keep a schedule you can maximize your time and in turn your productivity. I keep track of when my meals should be, when any appointments I have are, and I block out times for reading and amusement. It really has changed my life and given me a sense of direction and control over my time as well as increased my productivity.

5. Be Positive

Positivity is a key component to a successful mindset. You must avoid negativity and negative people. Surround yourself with positive minds and encourage each other. You must also accept your shortcomings and your strengths and build upon them. You cannot be positive if you do not accept your flaws.

Also, do not view others success as luck or good fortune, rather view it as inspiration. Learn from them rather than look down or demean them. If you find yourself looking down on others then you are far from success. Positivity is contagious and where it is success usually lives.

6. Study others who were successful

Many times as a human being we think that out problems are our own. That nobody else has ever faced our situation. I used to think that and I found out that thinking was flawed. There have been many people before us who have faced similar if not the exact same problems we have. With the internet it is easier than ever to look these people up and check out their life story.

Once you start reading about successful people you will be amazed to find the similarities with your own life. Many successful people had to go through many hardships to get where they wanted to go. You and I will be no different.

7. Be on the lookout for opportunities

This is another point which is paramount to becoming successful. Many people simply do not notice opportunities when they are presented with them. Now this happens for many reasons, but the main reason why people miss opportunities is because they are not paying attention to their surroundings. Today, many people have their heads buried in their phone or their heads filled with ear buds and their favorite music.

Now, there is nothing wrong with this as I also love to listen to my favorite music sometimes. But you have to realize that you may be missing valuable opportunities. Once you begin to notice your surroundings, opportunities will present themselves from every angle.

If you start to follow these tips you WILL optimize yourself for success. You will not achieve success right away, but you will put yourself in the best position possible when opportunity comes knocking.

Chapter 9: Where are you on the Sigmoid Curve?

If you're asking what is the Sigmoid Curve then this section isn't just an introduction but also lets you understand how to know where you are on this "S" curve as shown on Figure 1.

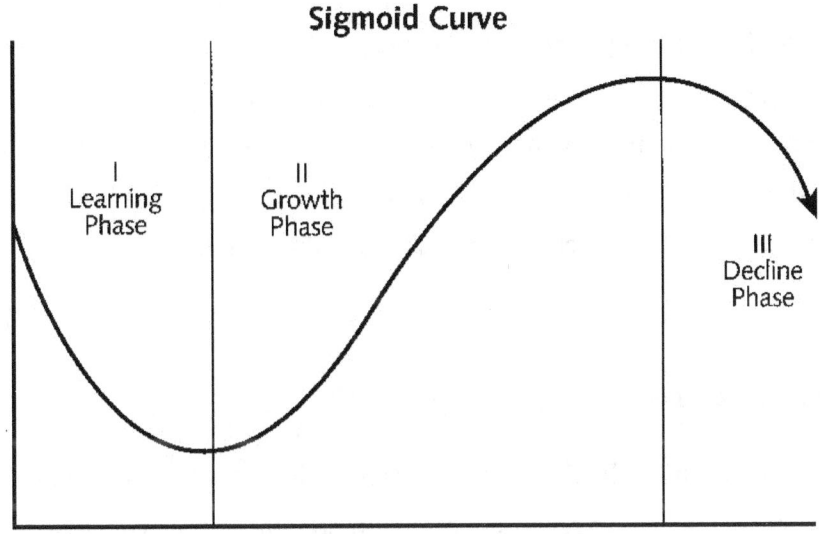

Figure 1

The Sigmoid Curve is the way Handy explains the need for organizations and individuals to manage change during the life cycle of an existing activity. All life cycles grow and decline in a bell-shaped curve. The secret, according to Handy, is to begin a new cycle as near to the top of the present cycle as can be predicted, i.e. before the peak when things start going downhill. With the vision and courage to start a new cycle before the peak, you have energy, time and resources while the existing cycle is running on automatic. The change model then stops being a simple one-off rise and fall but looks like a continuous "S", or "Sigmoid" curve.

The Sigmoid Curve is an expression of success over time. The success can be measured in terms of profit, money, power, influence. The object considered can be a country, a society, an individual, or a career.

Now let's look on more carefully with the phases of Sigmoid Curve from The Lesson of the Sigmoid Curve by SJW from Dumb Little Man.

The Sigmoid curve is a mathematical concept which has been widely used to model the natural life cycle of many things, from biological organisms, to schools and companies, marriages and careers. The curve is basically a stretched out S shape lying on its side, and can be thought of as having three sections, each of which corresponds to a phase of growth.

The Learning Phase

First, at the bottom of the S there is a section which rises slowly, often dipping before starting to rise (depending on how the curve is drawn). This corresponds to an initial period of learning. When someone starts a business or begins a new career (for example), there is a period of hard work, where little seems to get accomplished. Perhaps for several years, those involved work to make contacts, learn the right skills, and develop a roadmap for success.

This phase can be frustrating because so much effort is being expended with so little apparent result. You could compare it to sowing a crop and tending to the fields – for a long time, there is no sign of growth. But under the surface, something is happening. The seeds are developing, moving and growing.

Many businesses, careers and other ventures fail in this first phase because it is so hard to keep going with no tangible reward. We tend to be impatient and if we don't get some immediate reward for our efforts, we can move on to something else. But the only way to success is to push through this initial phase, to keep going and to know that this persistence will eventually and inevitably move on to phase two of the Sigmoid curve.

The Growth Phase

The second section is a sharply rising line in the elongated "S" shape. During this phase, business and careers move ahead quickly. Revenues increase, relationships mature, promotions occur easily, and organizations become much larger. This is where the crop which was sown is growing and coming to maturity, and every day brings perceptible growth and maturation.

The Decline Phase

The third phase of the curve is a decline, as the S shape starts to fall. The harvest has grown to maturity and starts to die. Morale and energy dip, revenues decline, the empire starts to crumble. On a personal level, your marriage might start to become jaded or you might wonder if you have chosen the right career or question how you are spending your time.

Surfing the Sigmoid Curve

Successful individuals and organizations are self-reflective and constantly monitor their own position on the sigmoid curve. However, to be truly successful is to go even further – it is to jump off the current curve when it is nearing its peak and start on the bottom of another curve. This can be very hard to do, because just as you are reaping the rewards of your work and application, you find yourself at the bottom of another learning curve.

This entails more pain, since growth always involves pain to some degree. It doesn't appear to make sense to change just as you are doing so well, reaping the rewards of your efforts. There is even, perhaps, a sense of loss – why throw away something which is mature and bringing a reward for something untested and new?

However, the most successful among us know that the alternative is an inevitable decline through phase three of the curve. Successful people are regularly reinventing themselves, their careers and their relationships, rising to new challenges and pushing through painful new phases of growth. The junction between the first and second is not easy or clean.

There is always a period of confusion, where the first curve is being abandoned and the second one embraced. This is a time of overlap, or ambiguity and of confusion.

When can you tell that it's time to jump off the first curve? This is an impossible question to answer, but the best advice is that it must always be assumed that the first curve is nearing a peak and preparation for the new curve should be underway. It may be that the first curve is longer than was thought, in which case you can keep cruising along until you are indeed nearer to the peak. But preparing for the second curve too early is far better than waiting until it is too late and the decline has set in. If you reach phase three before jumping off, you won't have the energy and the enthusiasm to make the change so easily and there is less chance of success.

Riding the first curve while cultivating the second is always the best option. Clinging to the first and trying to prolong it is a pointless waste of energy. When all is well and you are at the top of your game, then you know it is time to plan your exit.

Let's get deeper with the inevitable "dip" during Inception wonderfully presented by Kerwin Steffen, "The Sigmoid Growth Curve: Challenge and Assurance."

During the Inception Phase of a new growth curve, the organization almost always experiences a dip, an apparent setback. There's a temporary but real and sometimes alarming drop in resources and a sagging energy, effectiveness, and productivity on the part of work teams and individuals.

Parents of newborn babies know from experience that before an infant begins to grow following birth, it actually loses weight for a time. This can be alarming for a new Mom and Dad unless they have been told to expect this normal dip in weight.

Likewise, as organizations encounter changes or embark on new initiatives, they need to recognize that when they are in the Inception Phase of a growth curve they will experience a temporary dip. And people throughout the organization will do well to remind one another that such a dip is normal.

Every new growth curve (each new effort and even each small change in the goals or makeup of a group) triggers another Inception Phase with its characteristic dip and its accompanying anxiety.

On the positive side, that dip during the Inception Phase is akin to flexing your knees before you jump over a physical obstacle. By temporarily squatting (dipping), you can jump much higher and farther than you could with your knees straight.

The challenge of coexisting curves

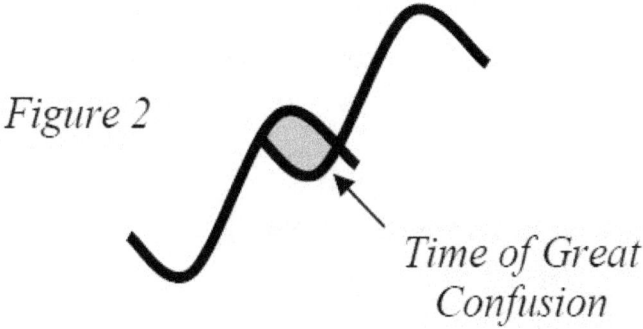

Figure 2

Time of Great Confusion

Even so, this dip presents a significant challenge. As shown in Figure 2, whenever an organization begins a new growth curve, the new and old curves must coexist for a time, as indicated by the shaded area. Experts have named this period the Time of Great Confusion.

The organization needs visionary, entrepreneurial leadership and an optimistic, courageous group spirit during this period, in order to:

- Manage the chaos, confusion, denial, and inevitable tension of sustaining both curves during that period when you are preparing to let go of the older one. (This can be a very traumatic time for those who have a stake in the old curve. They may strongly resist the new curve with its changes.)

- Remain open to constant questioning, learning, and adjusting as the group navigates its way through new, uncharted territory.

- Summon the confidence and the discipline (a) to allow resources to be pulled from the old curve (i.e., the "tried and true" way of doing things) and applied to the new, unproven one and (b) to develop totally new resources to support the new growth curve.

Courage to start a new Growth Curve

One final note: The secret to continue growth in an organization is to start a new sigmoid curve before the old one goes over the hump and plummets downhill to its demise.

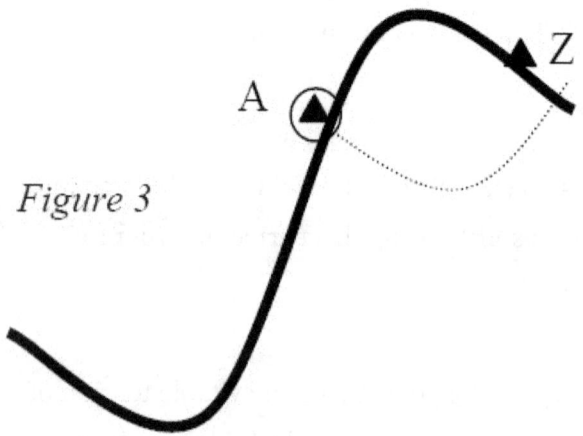

Figure 3

The highest point on any existing sigmoid curve from which a new curve is likely take off successfully is during the Maturity Phase and is indicated by Point A in Figure 3. This is usually the latest point at which there are still time, resources, and energy to get the new curve through its initial faltering uncertainty before the old curve has turned the corner (Point Z) and begun its inevitable slide to oblivion.

Chapter 10: Know Thy Business

> *"If A is success in life, then A = x + y + z.*
> *Work is x, play is y and z is keeping your mouth shut."*
> *– Albert Einstein*

This simple equation may show exactly what it takes to be successful in life, but the same is true for business. Loads of hard work and determination are necessary to make any given venture a success, particularly when speaking about business. That's why knowing your business is vital for success.

But, before knowing what kind of business you want then you should know whether you are capable for it or not. Here is a great checklist provided by Nicole Robinson, CEO, Gloss and Glam adapted from Forbes "Five Things You Should Know Before Starting A Business".

Save yourself countless hours — and the possible headache of making a huge foundational mistake — by getting these five things straight before you start up:

- Own your name. Make sure the company name you choose is one with an available trademark and Internet domain name. To see if a trademark is available, you can do a trademark search online through the United States Patent and Trademark Office's website.

Failure to properly obtain a trademark could put your fledgling business at risk — not to mention that the time and money you have invested in establishing your business name could go to waste if someone else owns the trademark. Don't assume your new business name is not trademarked because you were unsuccessful finding such name on the Internet, either. Someone could have used the name for a business that closed, or filed a trademark and never used it.

- Get in with the law. Understand what regulations, licenses and taxes you will need to follow, obtain and pay for your new business. After doing some initial research on your own, consult with a lawyer and accountant to confirm your understanding and to help structure your business to be in compliance with the law. Generally speaking, you will need to (i) ensure you are charging the correct amount of tax your service or product that your business is promoting, if applicable and (ii) obtain all of the proper licenses needed to run your new business, at a minimum. Establishing a successful business is hard enough. The last thing you need is some technical legality or administrative detail to stand in the way of your success.

- How much do you need to live? When working on your business plan, do not forget about the most important factor: YOU. You need to take into account your living costs. Rent, mortgages, and health insurance — these are all things that don't pay for themselves. You will most likely need to cut out all the unnecessary extras you can live without. Make sure you account for unforeseen or unexpected expenses by factoring a little flexibility into your budget for those "just-in-case" moments. You might even consider taking a part-time job until things pick up with your new venture and speak to a financial planner to help you budget yourself properly.

- Where are you in your life? Starting a new business takes brains, bravery, and what will seem to be endless hours of hard work. When you own your own company, there is always something that has to get done. You will most likely find yourself working at least 60-80 hours a week for the first two years. With that said, I'll ask you one very important question: Are you ready to give up your personal life for the next three years?

- Don't over — or under — spend. Starting a business can be incredibly financially taxing on you and your family. You will need to learn where and when to spend. It's important not to waste those precious seed dollars but it's equally important to spend where necessary. In any business, you often have to spend money to make money. Don't skimp out on things your company needs. For example, it may be worth it to put $1500 in an online vendor listing, but it may not be necessary to give every new customer a $15 mug. Be sure to keep up with technology too — there are many time-saving programs and apps (including free or inexpensive ones) that can help you keep track of it all, and as we all know, "time is money."

You've made the decision to start a business. Now you're asking yourself, "What type of business should I start?" Then What Type of Business Should You Start? And How to Choose the Right Type of Business by Susan Ward is the perfect piece for you.

You already know that there's a world of possibilities out there for anyone who wants to start a business. How can you possibly narrow them down to find the type of business that's right for you? The approach outlined in this section will help. Once you've worked your way through these five decisions, you will have a much better idea of exactly what type of business you want to start.

1) Retail or wholesale type of business?

Where do you want to be positioned on the supply chain? Retail businesses sell goods directly to consumers, usually in small quantities. Wholesalers buy goods (often in large quantities) from manufacturers or importers and then sell them to retailers and other distributors.

2) Franchise or independent type of business?

Many established companies offer franchises, which are basically copies of their companies. If you buy a franchise, you are buying the right to sell the parent company's goods and/or services in a specific area. Besides paying a franchise fee, you will also have to pay royalties and perhaps additional fees to the franchisor. You will also be expected to abide by the terms of the franchise agreement, which will often lay out exactly the way you will do business. Do some research to find some of the advantages and disadvantages of franchises and what to expect.

An independent business is one that you create and nurture on your own. Starting an independent business allows you the control and freedom that you won't get from a franchise operation.

3) Product or service (or mix of both) type of business?

If you are a trained professional, such as a dentist, accountant or realtor, your business is going to revolve around the professional services you can provide. But there are many professionals that also have the opportunity to offer related products, if they choose to do so. If you're a photographer, for example, you may decide to sell cameras, picture frames, and photo paper.

If you're not a trained professional, the key to deciding whether to focus on products or services when you're thinking about starting a business is determining where your true talents lie and what you most enjoy doing. Would you be happiest telling someone how to do something, doing something for them or offering them the products they would need to do the job themselves?

DO NOT base this decision on whether or not you enjoy selling or are good at it. No matter what type of business you start, you will be involved in sales.

4) Storefront or non-storefront type of business operation?

Finding the right business to start becomes much easier when you know exactly what you're looking for.

If you have decided to start a business selling products, you need a storefront of some kind, whether bricks-and-mortar, such as a retail store, or virtual, such as an e-commerce site. Many successful businesses have both, expanding their customers beyond their locale. Others "borrow" a storefront, so to speak, by getting their products distributed by other businesses, selling their products through markets and fairs, or by using available e-commerce venues. (Selling on eBay is one example of this.)

If you have decided to start a business selling services, you may or may not want a storefront. Many different services are actually performed at a customer's home, from cleaning through landscaping. While you would still need an office (either in your home or elsewhere), an actual storefront is unnecessary.

Some services can be offered over the phone or the Internet, such as the services offered by Virtual Assistants or some business coaches. These businesses often depend on virtual storefronts (business web sites) to attract clients.

Another option is to use your home as a storefront. While B&Bs are the obvious example of this, there are many other services that can operate successfully as home-based businesses, from travel agents through hairdressing.

5) In which industry/topic?

To make it easier on yourself, choose an industry or topic that you are not only interested in but have some expertise or experience. Otherwise, you're going to have to spend a lot of time and money educating yourself that you could be putting into your new business, or worse, making costly mistakes because you don't have the necessary knowledge.

Chapter 11: Psychology of Sales

"Help others achieve their dreams and
you will achieve yours."
– Les Brown

Have you ever wondered how other businesses sell more, even though your prices are better? There is actually a psychology behind it. We'll be referencing Robert Cialdini's Psychology of Persuasion. An article from Shopify by Mark Macdonald, 6 Psychological Triggers that Win Sales and Influence Customers explains it all.

As a professor of psychology and marketing, Cialdini lays out six ways you can get people to say yes to what you're asking. Anyone who sells things for a living, online or offline, should know, love, and live these principles:

- Reciprocity

- Commitment & Consistency

- Liking

- Authority

- Social Proof

- Scarcity

Let's take a look at how you can bring some of these influence triggers into your online store/business to start getting more sales and customers.

1. Reciprocity

The principle of reciprocity means that when someone gives us something we feel compelled to give something back in return. Have you ever gone to Costco and ended up with an unplanned sausage purchase in your cart because you felt a nagging obligation to buy because you tried a free sample? Well, that was the principle of reciprocity in action.

Of course, online retailers can't personally visit the house of each person who interacts with them to shove a sample in their hand. So how can you make reciprocity work for you?

Free Gift with Purchase

You might not be able to offer something in advance, but you can definitely offer something alongside. This tactic is a favorite of cosmetic and beauty products as demonstrated below by Ultra Beauty.

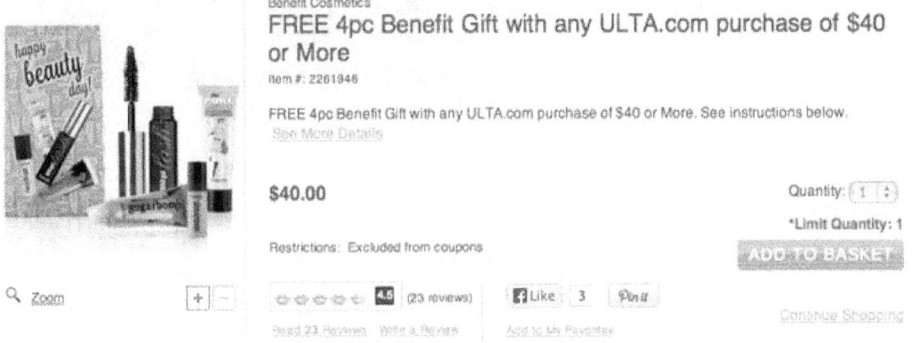

Even if you don't advertise the gift in advance, slipping samples of other products into your shipped product can create the feeling of having received a gift that might earn you a second purchase.

The Gift of Content

Content can be a good way for online retailers to provide value to potential customers—in effect, giving them a gift. For example, StyleSeek presents new users with a fun quiz they can go through to reach recommendations for clothes that match what they like:

True & Co, an online lingerie retailer, helps women figure out the right size and style of bra for them:

This fit quiz will help us stock your personal lingerie shop. First, bras: How are your shoulder straps?

○ SLIPPING OFF/SLIP SLIDING

○ DIGGING IN

○ THEY ARE FINE

So whether it's a guide for how to make the perfect vinaigrette or an exclusive author interview, use content as an ethical bribe that makes people feel grateful towards your business.

2. Commitment & Consistency

The principle of commitment and consistency says that people will go to great lengths to appear consistent in their words and actions - even to the extent of doing things that are basically irrational.

That's why if you're trying to make a change in your life - losing weight, for example - it can be very helpful to state your goal publicly. Once you've committed out loud (or online) you will have much more incentive to keep up your end of the bargain.

As a retailer, if you can get customers to make a small commitment to your brand (like signing up for your email newsletter), they are more likely to eventually purchase from you. And if you can actually get products in their hand, even if there is no official commitment to buy them, your chances increase even more.

This is the principle behind Warby Parker's Home Try-On Program:

Warby Parker knows that with a product that sits right in the middle of your face all day, look and fit are important. They also know that if they can get a set of frames in your hands, they are probably about 50% of the way to making a sale. So they make it as frictionless as possible - order the samples, get the box, order the frames you want, and send the box back for free. They say there's no commitment, but they are wise students of Cialdini - they know the customer feels the commitment the minute they open the box.

Zappos' famous easy return policy is another example of this - there is less friction for the customer to buy because they know that if they don't like it they can return it. But once they have the product in their hands, will they really return it? Probably not. They're already committed.

3. Liking

The principle of liking says that we are more likely to say yes to a request if we feel a connection to the person making it. That's why the sausage sample lady at Costco is always giving you a nice smile.

It's also why brands hire celebrities to endorse their products - so that people will transfer their love of Roger Federer to watches he's endorsing.

There are lots of ways to make this principle work for your store or business:

Telling Your Story

As a direct-response marketer I tend not to truck much with branding. But if there's one place that branding is essential, it is in triggering the principle of liking.

Every element of your store - colors, fonts, photo styles, copy - contributes to your brand personality, and your goal is to create a personality that is cohesive and that your target customer will like. This might be brisk and efficient if you are selling into a business market, warm and playful if you're selling children's products, earth tones and motherly if you're selling natural products.

Many stores will include something like an "About Us" page that is basically brand personality distilled. Here's an example from Hiut Denim Co:

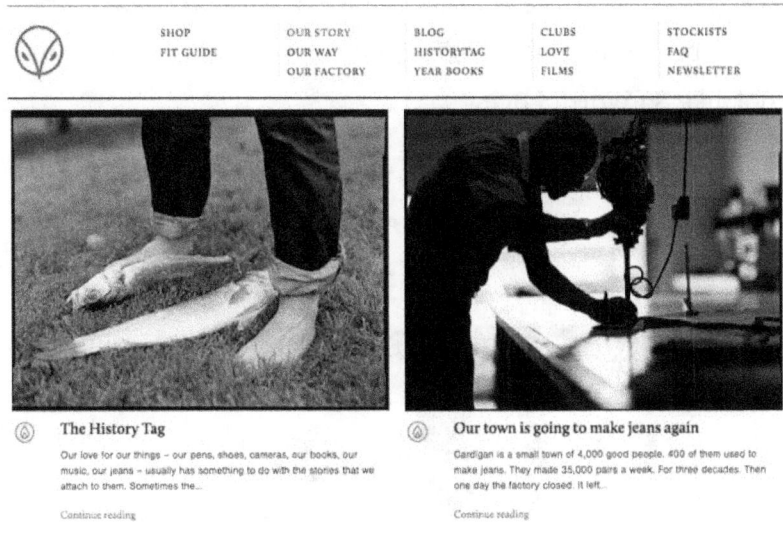

And one from jewelry designer Elva Fields:

This is a great way to sum up your story and to get people to like you.

Use Models People Can Identify With

If you're selling clothing, jewelry, or accessories, one quick way to create a connection to your customer is to show your stuff on people they will identify with and like. This doesn't mean you need to book Russian supermodels; it's best if they look like your customers. This might mean funky and cool, like So Worth Loving:

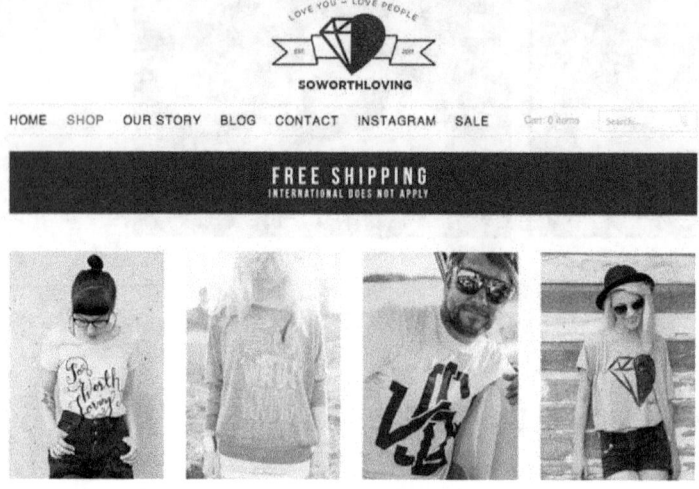

Casual and athletic, like Title Nine:

Social Links

People are more likely to purchase something if it's recommended to them by someone they know and trust. So make sure that your product pages have links to Twitter, Facebook, Pinterest, and Google+ so that your customers can tell their friends about the great product they just found on your site.

I know this sounds obvious, but I had to poke around to find examples, especially with smaller stores. But tea shop Little Sparrow is doing it right:

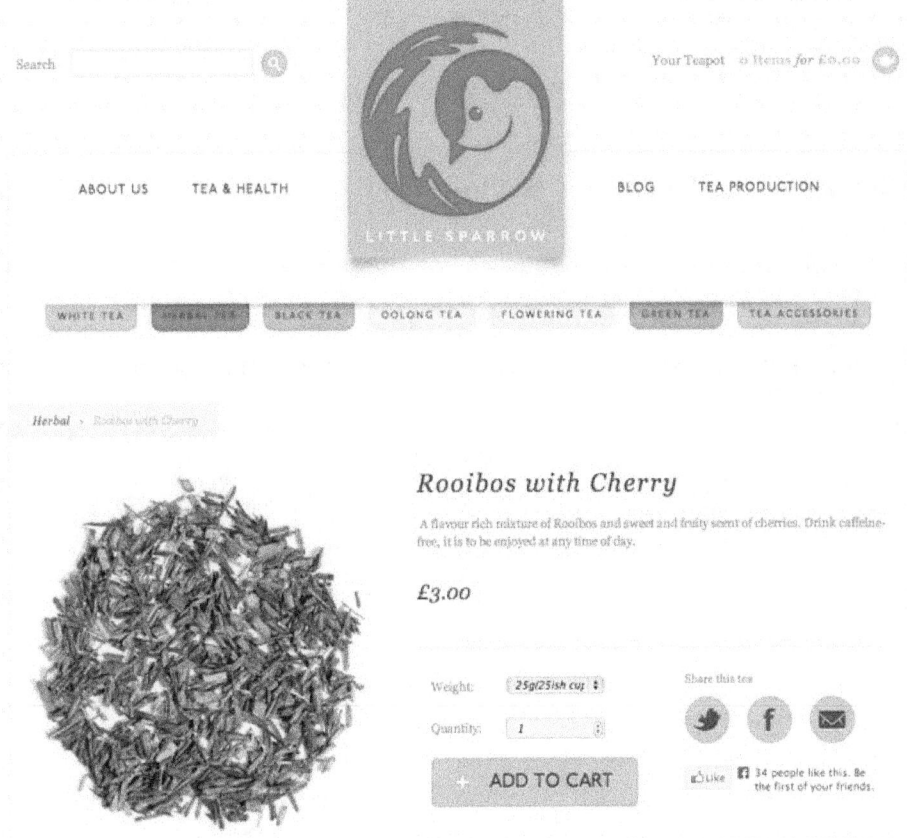

And so are more well-known brands, like Fab:

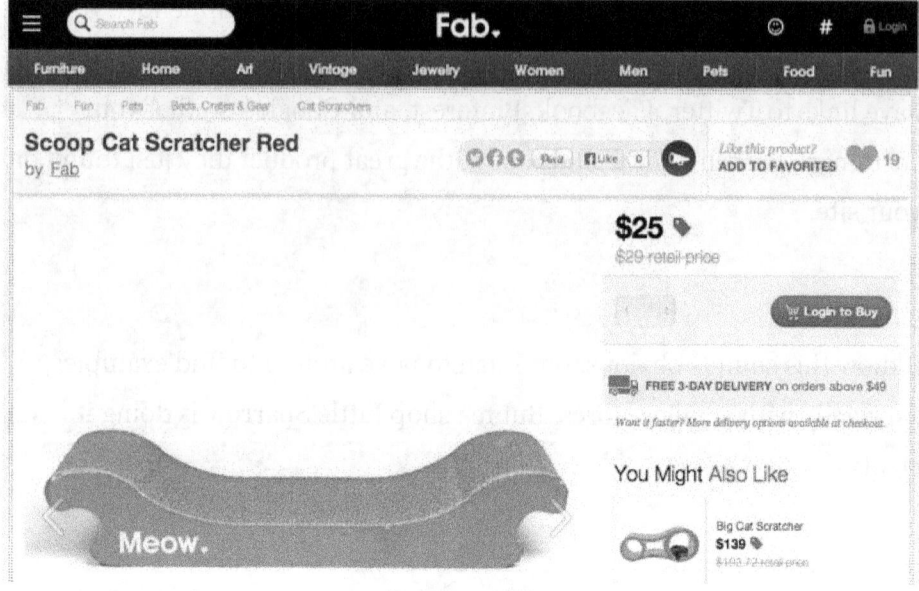

Display What Others Are Buying

Have you ever noticed someone wearing the same shoes or shirt as you and mentally saluted their fine taste? You probably felt a quick connection with that person based solely on that one data point.

Stores can play off that idea by presenting products that are similar to what the person is browsing, as seen here in the online store for the comic The Oatmeal:

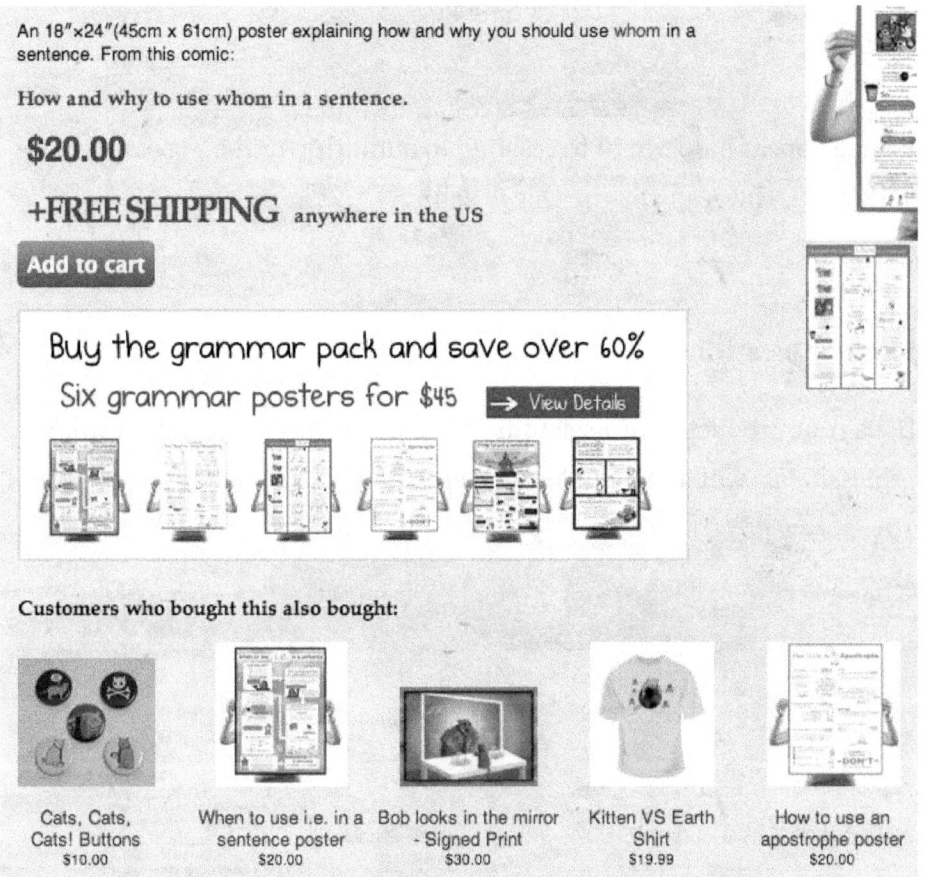

An 18"×24"(45cm x 61cm) poster explaining how and why you should use whom in a sentence. From this comic:

How and why to use whom in a sentence.

$20.00

+FREE SHIPPING anywhere in the US

Add to cart

Buy the grammar pack and save over 60%

Six grammar posters for $45   → View Details

Customers who bought this also bought:

Cats, Cats, Cats! Buttons	When to use i.e. in a sentence poster	Bob looks in the mirror - Signed Print	Kitten VS Earth Shirt	How to use an apostrophe poster
$10.00	$20.00	$30.00	$19.99	$20.00

4. Authority

Most people have heard of the famous Milgram experiments, in which volunteers were convinced to continue delivering what they thought were incredibly painful electric shocks to unseen subjects, even when they could hear (faked) screams of pain. The presence of a man in a lab coat telling them to continue was enough to earn the compliance of nearly all the volunteers.

People appear hard-wired to respond to authority (or the appearance of authority). How can you use this to sell?

Expert Creation

Does your product have a scientific secret sauce? Display content from professionals with credentials like Herbalife:

Is it hand-crafted by trained artisans? Tell the world all about them like Dodocase:

PRESERVING TRADITIONAL BOOKBINDING TECHNIQUES

The DODOcase philosophy is simple: make things locally and help keep the art of bookbinding alive and well by adapting it to a world of digital devices. Our skilled craftsmen make beautiful products to meet today's modern needs using age-old techniques that need preserving. It's a happy marriage of tradition and technology.

And of course books are another great example of this. Are you more likely to buy a run-of-the-mill book about how to cook French Food... or one by Jacques Pepin? Cookbook Village knows that big names sell books and they have a whole section for big name chefs:

Cookbook Village

VINTAGE AND USED COOKBOOKS FOR CHEFS, COLLECTORS AND FOODIES.

CONTACT   SUBSCRIBE   P: 480-583-8716   VIEW CART

HOME   COOKBOOKS ▾   BUZZ AND NEWS   COOKBOOK COLLECTING   ABOUT ▾   SUPPORT ▾

Home > Top Chef Cookbooks

TOP CHEF COOKBOOKS

As food-themed television entertainment continues to inspire cooks and chefs to become culinary masters, top chefs are publishing new cookbooks at each turn. This collection of cookbooks from celebrity chefs around the world is sure to take your cooking to new heights.

JOHN BESH COOKBOOK - MY FAMI...	JOHN ASH COOKBOOK - FROM EA...	URBAN ITALIAN COOKBOOK - AND...	MASTER CHEFS COOK KOSHER A...
$14.40	$11.70	$15.30	$13.50

Expert Curation

These days the range of products available to a shopper are so vast it's hard to wade through them all—and that's why "curation" has become the buzzword of the moment.

Do you have a Chief Stylist (or someone who could reasonably pass for that)? Have a page with her top picks for the season. Selling fitness products? Have a personal trainer give his/her favorite picks. Even a little authority is enough; Kepler's Books provides recommendations from each of their staff members:

5. Social Proof

The principle of social proof is connected to the principle of liking: because we are social creatures, we tend to like things just because other people do as well, whether we know them or not. Anything that shows the popularity of your site and your products can trigger a response.

Have you gotten good press? Mention it! Received loving emails from customers? Quote them! Gotten good feedback from your mom? Heck, get it up there. Look, cute tableware purveyor Camila Prada has done all three:

WELCOME TO CAMILAPRADA
THE CUTEST TABLEWARE
IN THE WORLD.
OUR MUMS SAID SO!

MADE ENTIRELY
IN BRITAIN

AS SEEN IN:

 INSIDE

 apartment therapy

GRAND DESIGNS

 design

 ANORAK

WHAT PEOPLE ARE SAYING:

"Just wanted to say thank you for your excellent customer service! Momo arrived today and was welcomed by the rest of the gang, I love my colourful kitchen creatures."

Janne Sund, Norway.

Another tactic is to provide a "Best Sellers" or "Most Popular" page, as demonstrated by Black Milk below. Are the anatomically-correct muscle leggings really their most popular, or just the ones that are most piled up in the warehouse? As a consumer, I don't know. But by declaring these particular leggings the most wanted, Black Milk has given them a boost of desirability.

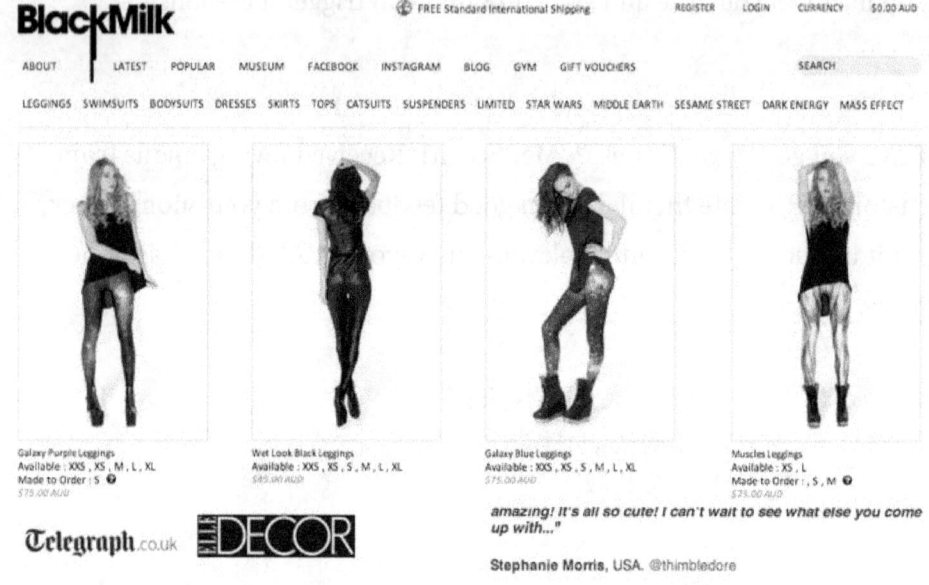

And of course, ratings and reviews, like Amazon & countless other retailers, are another fine way to show social proof.

6. Scarcity

Cialdini's final principle is the principle of scarcity, which states that people are highly motivated by the thought that they might lose out on something. Call it the Eternal Teenager Principle: if someone tells you that you can't have it - boy, do you want it. This is probably the one I'm the biggest sucker for, personally.

Marketers trigger this effect by using all kinds of tactics to suggest that products (or low prices) might soon be gone, or that someone is trying to keep this product off the market.

Deadlines for Sales

Lily Pulitzer is counting down to the seconds to when her summer sale prices will become unavailable.

Impending Out-Of-Stock Announcements

You want that cute toy box from ModMom? Well, you'd better hurry - there are only three left!

Seasonal or Limited Products

Every March when my friend gets her green Shamrock Shake from McDonalds she crows with happiness all over the social media. Think she'd be that excited if she could walk in and get it any time? Of course not. The knowledge that the supply is limited motivates her—and makes her feel like a success for having "won."

And speaking of me being a sucker for this tactic, that's exactly how I feel about my Pumpkin Spice Latte from Starbucks.

How do you know
It's Fall?

Everyone has their favorite #itsfallwhen moments.
Let's hear yours.

Feeling the crunch of leaves under your
feet while enjoying the sweet goodness
of a Pumpkin Spice Latte.

Cozying up at home by the fire.

But What About Pricing?

You may be wondering where the extremely common retail tactics of sales & discounts fall under these six principles. Is Cialdini saying that price doesn't impact people's purchasing behavior?

Of course it does, and Cialdini mentions a couple of pricing experiments in the beginning of his book. But think of it this way: the price of your product represents the size of a risk someone is going to take on. In other words, people will be a lot more choosey over a $10,000 product than one that is $1.

Risk Removal

The six principles of influence represent additional non-obvious ways to impact perceived risk. For example, by using appeals to authority, you're decreasing the risk of a 'yes' - someone who says yes (to your appeal to buy a product) can always point to the authority you've demonstrated to rationalize their purchase. By using scarcity tactics, you're increasing the risk of a 'no' - someone who declines your offer right now might miss out.

So given a price that you have settled on for your products, using the principles of influence can decrease the risk of 'yes' (liking, social proof, authority) or increase the risk of 'no' (scarcity, consistency, reciprocity).

Sprinkle them throughout your site and watch your sales go up!

Chapter 12: Personal Strategic Plan

"If we did all the things we are capable of, we would literally astound ourselves." – Thomas Edison

Strategic planning is the process executives undertake in order to make thoughtful decisions about their organization's mission, values and goals, and properly allocate resources to fulfill those directives. Therefore when we say personal strategic plan, it's all about knowing yourself and knowing what you are capable of. In an article by Brian Tracy, Personal Strategic Planning: 4-step action plan to strengthen your personal skills, we'll discover his amazing 4 steps of personal strategic planning.

Only by discovering your innate, personal skills and developing and exploiting them to their highest degree can you utilize yourself to get the greatest amount of satisfaction and enjoyment from everything you do. Creating an action plan through personal strategic planning can give you the highest rewards for your efforts and is the starting point in getting the best out of yourself.

CORPORATE VS. PERSONAL STRATEGIC PLANNING

When we do strategic planning for corporations, we begin with the premise that the whole purpose of the exercise is to reorganize and reallocate people and resources to increase the rate of return on equity, or capital invested in the business. Invariably, this is done by emphasizing some areas and de-emphasizing others, by allocating more resources to areas with higher potential return and by taking resources away from those areas that represent lower potential returns. By developing or promoting newer and better products and services and by discontinuing those products and services that are less profitable, the company and all the people in it can channel their resources to maximize their returns.

In doing personal strategic planning, the first thing you want to think about is increasing your personal "return on energy," rather than return on equity. You need to realize that the most essential and valuable thing that you have to bring to your life and to your work is your ability to think, to act and to get results. You're earning ability—which is a function of your education, knowledge, experience and talents—is your human capital, or your equity. And the way you develop your personal skills and use your earning ability will largely determine the quality and quantity of your rewards, both material and psychological, both tangible and intangible.

ACTION PLAN STEP 1 :
CLARIFY YOUR VALUES

This first part of personal strategic planning is called "values clarification." You ask yourself, "What values and virtues do I most admire and wish to practice in my life?" If you wanted to discover your strengths and personal skills in the work world, first you would define your values as they apply to employment. The values that companies settle upon would be similar to the values that you organize your work life around. Often, both companies and individuals will choose values such as integrity, quality, respect for others, service, profitability, innovation, entrepreneurship, market leadership, and so on.

In a similar vein, you could use those values to define your position with regard to your work. In your personal strategic planning, you could decide to plan your work life around the values of quality, excellence, service, profitability, and innovation. There are dozens of values that you can pick from, but whichever you choose, and the order of priority you place on your choices, will determine your approach to your work.

ACTION PLAN STEP 2 :
CREATE YOUR PERSONAL MISSION STATEMENT

Your next step is to create your personal mission statement. This is a clear, written description of the person you intend to be in your work life. I have often found that this is even more important than setting specific financial or business or sales goals. Once you have decided how much you want to earn, you need to write out a personal mission statement that describes the kind of person you intend to become in order to earn that amount of money.

Remember: Your goal is to identify your personal skills and strengths so that you can deploy yourself in such a way as to increase your personal return on energy. In personal strategic planning, one of the best mental techniques that you can use to develop your personal skills is to see yourself as a "bundle of resources" that can be applied in a variety of directions to achieve a variety of objectives. As a bundle of resources, the amount of time and energy that you have is limited; therefore, your time and energy must be put to their highest and best use. Stand back and imagine that you're looking at yourself objectively, as if through the eyes of another person, and you're thinking about how you could apply yourself to bring about the best results. See yourself as your own employer or boss. What could you do to maximize the output of which you're capable, and where could you do it?

ACTION PLAN STEP 3 :
PERFORM AN AUDIT TO STRENGTHEN PERSONAL SKILLS

Once you have defined your values and written out your mission statement, the next step of personal strategic planning is to do what is called a "situational analysis." Sometimes we call it a "performance audit." This is the process of analyzing yourself thoroughly before you begin setting specific goals and planning certain activities. You begin your performance audit by asking yourself some key questions.

One of those questions should be, "What are my marketable skills?" Think about it. What can you do for which someone else will pay you? What can you do particularly well? What can you do better than others? What have you done particularly well in the past?

A wage or a salary is merely an amount of money that is paid to purchase a certain quality and quantity of labor or output. The results that you're able to get by applying your personal skills and strengths largely determine your rewards in life. If you wish to increase the quality and quantity of your rewards, you have to increase your ability to achieve more and better results. It's very simple.

ACTION PLAN STEP 4 :
DETERMINE YOUR AREA OF EXCELLENCE

Finally, in personal strategic planning, the aim is always to achieve leadership in your chosen market niche. Business leaders have the authority to determine the area of excellence in their business. Analogously, on a personal level, you can choose the thing at which you're going to become absolutely excellent and achieve extraordinary results. So in what areas are you going to work to achieve results that are far beyond what the average person could be expected to accomplish?

You were put on this earth with a special combination of talents, abilities, and personal skills that make you different from anyone who has ever lived. Whatever you're doing today, it's nowhere near what you're really capable of doing. The key to a happy and prosperous life is for you to regularly evaluate your strengths and weaknesses, to become very good in the areas you most enjoy, and then to throw your whole heart into what you're doing.

Chapter 13: Study the Competition

Your competition is businesses in the same industry. It is important to learn and understand them because not only can it help you improve your business but make it flourish and better. Info Entrepreneur, a Canada business network, showed a good list and answered many "why" questions of studying your competition on their guide Understand Your Competitors.

Knowing who your competitors are, and what they are offering, can help you to make your products, services and marketing stand out. It will enable you to set your prices competitively and help you to respond to rival marketing campaigns with your own initiatives.

You can use this knowledge to create marketing strategies that take advantage of your competitors' weaknesses, and improve your own business performance. You can also assess any threats posed by both new entrants to your market and current competitors. This knowledge will help you to be realistic about how successful you can be.

This chapter explains how to analyze who your competitors are, how to research what they're doing and how to act on the information you gain.

- Who are your competitors?

- What you need to know about your competitors

- Learning about your competitors

- Hearing about your competitors

- How to act on the competitor information you get

WHO ARE YOUR COMPETITORS?

All businesses face competition. Even if you're the only restaurant in town you must compete with cinemas, bars and other businesses where your customers will spend their money instead of with you. With increased use of the Internet to buy goods and services and to find places to go, you are no longer just competing with your immediate neighbors. Indeed, you could find yourself competing with businesses from other countries.

Your competitor could be a new business offering a substitute or similar product that makes your own redundant.

Competition is not just another business that might take money away from you. It can be another product or service that's being developed and which you ought to be selling or looking to license before somebody else takes it up.

And don't just research what's already out there. You also need to be constantly on the lookout for possible new competition.

You can get clues to the existence of competitors from:

- local business directories
- your local Chamber of Commerce
- advertising
- press reports
- exhibitions and trade fairs
- questionnaires
- searching on the Internet for similar products or services
- information provided by customers
- flyers and marketing literature that have been sent to you - quite common if you're on a bought-in marketing list
- searching for existing patented products that are similar to yours
- planning applications and building work in progress

WHAT YOU NEED TO KNOW ABOUT YOUR COMPETITORS

Monitor the way your competitors do business. Look at:

- the products or services they provide and how they market them to customers

- the prices they charge

- how they distribute and deliver

- the devices they employ to enhance customer loyalty and what back-up service they offer

- their brand and design values

- whether they innovate - business methods as well as products

- their staff numbers and the calibre of staff that they attract

- how they use IT - for example, if they're technology-aware and offer a website and email

- who owns the business and what sort of person they are

- their annual report - if they're a public company

- their media activities - check their website as well as local newspapers, radio, television and any outdoor advertising

How they treat their customers

Find out as much as possible about your competitors' customers, such as:

- who they are

- what products or services different customers buy from them

- what customers see as your competitors' strengths and weaknesses

- whether there are any long-standing customers

- if they've had an influx of customers recently

What they're planning to do

Try to go beyond what's happening now by investigating your competitors' business strategy, for example:

- what types of customer they're targeting

- what new products they're developing

- what financial resources they have

LEARNING ABOUT YOUR COMPETITORS

Read about your competitors. Look for articles or ads in the trade press or mainstream publications. Read their marketing literature. Check their entries in directories and phone books. If they are an online business, ask for a trial of their service.

Are they getting more publicity than you, perhaps through networking or sponsoring events? If your competitor is a public company, read a copy of their annual report.

Go to exhibitions

At exhibitions and trade fairs check which of your competitors are also exhibiting. Look at their stands and promotional activities. Note how busy they are and who visits them.

Go online

Look at competitors' websites. Find out how they compare to yours. Check any interactive parts of the site to see if you could improve on it for your own website. Is the information free of charge? Is it easy to find?

Business websites often give much information that businesses haven't traditionally revealed - from the history of the company to biographies of the staff.

Use a search engine to track down similar products. Find out who else offers them and how they go about it.

Websites can give you good tips on what businesses around the globe are doing in your industry sector.

Organizations and reference sources

- Your trade or professional association, if applicable.

- The local Chamber of Commerce.

- Directories and survey reports in any business reference library.

HEARING ABOUT YOUR COMPETITORS

Speak to your competitors. Phone them to ask for a copy of their brochure or get one of your staff or a friend to drop by and pick up their marketing literature.

You could ask for a price list or inquire what an off-the-shelf item might cost and if there's a discount for volume. This will give you an idea at which point a competitor will discount and at what volume.

Phone and face-to-face contacts will also give you an idea of the style of the company, the quality of their literature and the initial impressions they make on customers.

It's also likely you'll meet competitors at social and business events. Talk to them. Be friendly - they're competitors not enemies. You'll get a better idea of them - and you might need each other one day, for example in collaborating to grow a new market for a new product.

Listen to your customers and suppliers

Make the most of contacts with your customers. Don't just ask how well you're performing - ask which of your competitors they buy from and how you compare.

Use meetings with your suppliers to ask what their other customers are doing. They may not tell you everything you want to know, but it's a useful start.

Use your judgement with any information they volunteer. For instance, when customers say your prices are higher than the competition they may just be trying to negotiate a better deal.

HOW TO ACT ON THE COMPETITOR INFORMATION YOU GET

Evaluate the information you find about your competitors. This should tell you whether there are gaps in the market you can exploit. It should also indicate whether there is a saturation of suppliers in certain areas of your market, which might lead you to focus on less competitive areas. Draw up a list of everything that you've found out about your competitors, however small.

Put the information into three categories:

- what you can learn from and do better

- what they're doing worse than you

- what they're doing the same as you

What you can learn from and do better

If you're sure your competitors are doing something better than you, you need to respond and make some changes. It could be anything from improving customer service, assessing your prices and updating your products, to changing the way you market yourself, redesigning your literature and website and changing your suppliers.

Try to innovate not imitate. Now you've got the idea, can you do it even better, add more value?

Your competitors might not have rights over their actual ideas, but remember the rules on patents, copyright and design rights.

What they're doing worse than you

Exploit the gaps you've identified. These may be in their product range or service, marketing or distribution, even the way they recruit and retain employees.

Customer service reputation can often provide the difference between businesses that operate in a very competitive market. Renew your efforts in these areas to exploit the deficiencies you've discovered in your competitors.

But don't be complacent about your current strengths. Your current offerings may still need improving and your competitors may also be assessing you. They may adopt and enhance your good ideas.

What they're doing the same as you

Why are they doing the same as you, particularly if you're not impressed by other things they do? Perhaps you both need to make some changes.

Analyze these common areas and see whether you've got it right. And even if you have, your competitor may be planning an improvement.

Chapter 14: "Hustle, while you wait"- Thomas Edison

"Everything comes to those who hustle while they wait."
– Thomas Edison

Let's learn something about this quote by Thomas Edison from Julie Holland on her EzineArticles post, "Hustle While You Wait"

Thomas A. Edison was one of the most prolific inventors of all time. His inventions continue to shape our daily lives decades after his death in 1931. He fundamentally changed our lives by giving us indoor lighting, records, movies, batteries, and hundreds of other objects we have come to believe we can't live without. He patented over 1,000 objects during his life. His advice to "hustle" while you wait gives us some insight into how he became a legend.

Many people who dream of changing their lives are in a "waiting" time in their lives. For financial or personal reasons they are not yet able to leave their current jobs, move to their preferred geographical area, or start that business they dream of. During these waiting times you can do much to lay the foundation for your dreams. Here are some ideas that can get you started as you begin to move towards a life you compose rather than one you fell into:

Research your dream job or business.

Learn all that you can about it. You can easily become an expert about any topic in 3-6 months. Read, search the web, interview people who already work in the field, and do all that you can to learn about the history, trends and topics that are important in your field. When the time comes to move forward, you will have a solid knowledge base.

Develop your network.

Meet others who are in your chosen field. Nothing leads to success faster than having a solid support network in place. Don't fear competition; just meet as many people as you can in that field. This networking will help you understand what it takes to succeed and give you the support you need to make those first steps. Nothing increases learning faster than having a mentor who can show you the way. You will increase your confidence and learning pace, and you may even get "lucky" and find a job or your first client.

Lay the groundwork.

Write your business plan. Draft a press release. Outline your book. Learn how to design web pages. Any progress is movement forward and that momentum can help propel you towards the life of your dreams. As you develop skills and create the platform for your new life, new ideas and opportunities will come your way.

No matter where you are in developing the life of your dreams, you can "hustle" while you wait. Even if you have no idea what you want yet, you can create a foundation that will support your new life. No effort is wasted. The skills and knowledge you gain will fit into your new life in some way.

Chapter 15: The Three P's of Marketing (People, Processes, and Product)

If you look it up, you'll end up with a different 3 P's of marketing and even up to 7 P's and extended strategies for marketing. In this chapter we'll focus with the 3 P's we need to evaluate properly and see why *people, processes* and *products* are the 3 P's we'll talk about.

The marketing mix is a business tool used in marketing. The term marketing mix was coined in an article written by Neil Borden called "The Concept of the Marketing Mix." In this mix is The 3 P's in Marketing, a strategy of proven techniques that many companies over the years have developed to become highly profitable in their markets. Following these concepts will guide you to success.

Here are the 3 P's PEOPLE, PROCESSES and PRODUCT. Even though over time it has expanded to 6 and 7 P's, we are starting with the basics and we will bring it back to how it relates helping your business through website design. (Freely adapted from RayvanBros, "The 3 P's of Marketing")

PEOPLE

We'll start with *people* because how can a business begin without a single person. People are all human actors who plays a part in service delivery and thus influence the buyers' perceptions; namely the firms personnel, the customer and other people in the service department. They are the one who provides cues to the customer regarding the nature of the service. (Junesh Acharya: A Powerpoint Presentation of the 3 P's of Service Marketing)

An extremely important part of any company is having the right people to support the company's products and/or service. Excellent customer service personnel who can provide support with clearly known expectations, such as hours of operation and average response time, is key to maintaining a high level of customer satisfaction as carefully explained by Entrepreneur on their "The 7 Ps of Marketing."

PROCESSES

Solid procedures and policies that are in place, which pertains to the company's products and/or service, is an extremely valuable element to the marketing strategy. Customers want to understand more than just your product; they also want to focus on the shape and form your business will take. This can also be called a promotion.

This includes all the ways you tell your customers about your products or services and how you then market and sell to them.

Small changes in the way you promote and sell your products can lead to dramatic changes in your results. Even small changes in your advertising can lead immediately to higher sales. Experienced copywriters can often increase the response rate from advertising by 500 percent by simply changing the headline on an advertisement.

Large and small companies in every industry continually experiment with different ways of advertising, promoting, and selling their products and services. And here is the rule: Whatever method of marketing and sales you're using today will, sooner or later, stop working. Sometimes it will stop working for reasons you know, and sometimes it will be for reasons you don't know. In either case, your methods of marketing and sales will eventually stop working, and you'll have to develop new sales, marketing and advertising approaches, offerings, and strategies.

PRODUCT

To begin with, develop the habit of looking at your product as though you were an outside marketing consultant brought in to help your company decide whether or not it's in the right business at this time. Ask critical questions such as, "Is your current product or service, or mix of products and services, appropriate and suitable for the market and the customers of today?"

Whenever you're having difficulty selling as much of your products or services as you'd like, you need to develop the habit of assessing your business honestly and asking, "Are these the right products or services for our customers today?"

Is there any product or service you're offering today that, knowing what you now know, you would not bring out again today? Compared to your competitors, is your product or service superior in some significant way to anything else available? If so, what is it? If not, could you develop an area of superiority? Should you be offering this product or service at all in the current marketplace?

As that said, we'll also include other P's of Marketing to broaden your understanding with it.

Prices

Develop the habit of continually examining and re-examining the prices of the products and services you sell to make sure they're still appropriate to the realities of the current market. Sometimes you need to lower your prices. At other times, it may be appropriate to raise your prices. Many companies have found that the profitability of certain products or services doesn't justify the amount of effort and resources that go into producing them. By raising their prices, they may lose a percentage of their customers, but the remaining percentage generates a profit on every sale. Could this be appropriate for you?

Sometimes you need to change your terms and conditions of sale. Sometimes, by spreading your price over a series of months or years, you can sell far more than you are today, and the interest you can charge will more than make up for the delay in cash receipts. Sometimes you can combine products and services together with special offers and special promotions. Sometimes you can include free additional items that cost you very little to produce but make your prices appear far more attractive to your customers.

In business, as in nature, whenever you experience resistance or frustration in any part of your sales or marketing plan, be open to revisiting that area. Be open to the possibility that your current pricing structure is not ideal for the current market. Be open to the need to revise your prices, if necessary, to remain competitive, to survive and thrive in a fast-changing marketplace.

Place

Place where your product or service is actually sold. Develop the habit of reviewing and reflecting upon the exact location where the customer meets the salesperson. Sometimes a change in place can lead to a rapid increase in sales.

You can sell your product in many different places. Some companies use direct selling, sending their salespeople out to personally meet and talk with the prospect. Some sell by telemarketing. Some sell through catalogs or mail order. Some sell at trade shows or in retail establishments. Some sell in joint ventures with other similar products or services. Some companies use manufacturers' representatives or distributors. Many companies use a combination of one or more of these methods.

In each case, the entrepreneur must make the right choice about the very best location or place for the customer to receive essential buying information on the product or service needed to make a buying decision. What is yours? In what way should you change it? Where else could you offer your products or services?

Chapter 16: Branding

What is branding? Well according to the Business Dictionary, branding is the process involved in creating a unique name and image for a product in the consumers' mind, mainly through advertising campaigns with a consistent theme. Branding aims to establish a significant and differentiated presence in the market that attracts and retains loyal customers.

According to Entrepreneur's The Basics of Branding article, Branding is one of the most important aspects of any business, large or small, retail or B2B. An effective brand strategy gives you a major edge in increasingly competitive markets. But what exactly does "branding" mean? How does it affect a small business like yours?

Simply put, your brand is your promise to your customer. It tells them what they can expect from your products and services, and it differentiates your offering from your competitors'. Your brand is derived from who you are, who you want to be and who people perceive you to be.

Are you the innovative maverick in your industry or the experienced, reliable one? Is your product the high-cost, high-quality option, or the low-cost, high-value option? You can't be both, and you can't be all things to all people. Who you are should be based to some extent on who your target customers want and need you to be.

The foundation of your brand is your logo. Your website, packaging and promotional materials--all of which should integrate your logo--communicate your brand.

Brand Strategy & Equity

Your brand strategy is how, what, where, when and to whom you plan on communicating and delivering on your brand messages. Where you advertise is part of your brand strategy. Your distribution channels are also part of your brand strategy. And what you communicate visually and verbally are part of your brand strategy, too.

Consistent, strategic branding leads to a strong brand equity, which means the added value brought to your company's products or services that allows you to charge more for your brand than what identical, unbranded products command. The most obvious example of this is Coke vs. a generic soda. Because Coca-Cola has built a powerful brand equity, it can charge more for its product--and customers will pay that higher price.

The added value intrinsic to brand equity frequently comes in the form of perceived quality or emotional attachment. For example, Nike associates its products with star athletes, hoping customers will transfer their emotional attachment from the athlete to the product. For Nike, it's not just the shoe's features that sell the shoe.

Defining Your Brand

Defining your brand is like a journey of business self-discovery. It can be difficult, time-consuming and uncomfortable. It requires, at the very least, that you answer the questions below:

- What is your company's mission?

- What are the benefits and features of your products or services?

- What do your customers and prospects already think of your company?

- What qualities do you want them to associate with your company?

Do your research. Learn the needs, habits and desires of your current and prospective customers. And don't rely on what you think they think. Know what they think.

Because defining your brand and developing a brand strategy can be complex, consider leveraging the expertise of a non-profit small-business advisory group.

Once you've defined your brand, how do you get the word out? Here are a few simple, time-tested tips:

- Get a great logo. Place it everywhere.

- Write down your brand messaging. What are the key messages you want to communicate about your brand? Every employee should be aware of your brand attributes.

- Integrate your brand. Branding extends to every aspect of your business--how you answer your phones, what you or your salespeople wear on sales calls, your e-mail signature, everything.

- Create a "voice" for your company that reflects your brand. This voice should be applied to all written communication and incorporated in the visual imagery of all materials, online and off. Is your brand friendly? Be conversational. Is it ritzy? Be more formal. You get the gist.

- Develop a tagline. Write a memorable, meaningful and concise statement that captures the essence of your brand.

- Design templates and create brand standards for your marketing materials. Use the same color scheme, logo placement, look and feel throughout. You don't need to be fancy, just consistent.

- Be true to your brand. Customers won't return to you--or refer you to someone else--if you don't deliver on your brand promise.

- Be consistent. I placed this point last only because it involves all of the above and is the most important tip I can give you. If you can't do this, your attempts at establishing a brand will fail.

And here are "Ten ways to build a brand for your small business" by The Market Donut.

1. Start by defining your brand.

   Review the product or service your business offers, pinpoint the space in the market it occupies and research the emotive and rational needs and concerns of your customers. Your brand character should promote your business, connect with your customer base and differentiate you in the market.

2. When building your brand, think of it as a person.

   Every one of us is an individual whose character is made up of beliefs, values and purposes that define who we are and who we connect with. Our personality determines how we behave in different situations, how we dress and what we say. Of course for people it's intuitive and it's rare that you even consider what your own character is, but when you're building a brand it's vital to have that understanding.

3. Consider what is driving your business.

   What does it believe in, what is its purpose and who are its brand heroes? These things can help establish your emotive brand positioning and inform the identity and character for brand communications.

4. Aim to build long-term relationships with your customers.

   Don't dress up your offering and raise expectations that result in broken promises, create trust with honest branding — be clear who your company is and be true to the values that drive it every day.

5. Speak to your customers with a consistent tone of voice.

   It will help reinforce the business's character and clarify its offering so customers are aware exactly what to expect from the product or service.

6. Don't repeat the same message in the same way over and over again. Alternatively, aim to make your key messages work together to build a coherent identity.

7. Don't try to mimic the look of chains or big brands.

   Try and carve out your own distinctive identity. There is a big consumer trend towards independent establishments, and several chains are in fact trying to mimic an independent feel to capture some of that market. Truly independent operators can leverage their status to attract customers who are looking for something more original and authentic, that aligns with how they feel about themselves.

8. Be innovative, bold and daring – stand for something you believe in.

    Big brands are encumbered by large layers of bureaucracy, preventing them from being flexible and reacting to the ever-changing needs of their customers. Those layers of decision-makers can make it hard for them to be daring with their branding.

9. Always consider your branding when communicating with customers.

    Don't lose your pride or dilute your brand positioning with indiscriminate discounting. Try offering more, rather than slashing prices. Promotions are an opportunity to reinforce your brand mission.

10. The old way of stamping your logo on everything won't cut it.

    The future of branding is fluid and engaging — respect your customers' intelligence by not giving everything away up front. Generate some intrigue and allow them to unearth more about your brand for themselves. This is the way to foster ambassadors who revel in telling other people what they have discovered.

Acknowledgements

I would like to thank everyone again that we mentioned in the credits and references, but we would also like to thank everyone that either bought this book, or used this book to make their business or themselves better.

Optimize ourselves and our business and we can optimize America. We can put American's back to work. We have to optimize our local communities. It is our responsibility, it is our duty, and it is our country.

God Bless America

I would like to thank the following for help with this book: Gene Helen Grier, Monique D. Hudson, Kay Johnson, Miqual Hudson and Google.com.

"If we did all the things we are capable of, we would literally astound ourselves."

– Thomas Edison

Credits

We would like to thank all those that contributed and participated in the development of this book. If you aren't certain that the principles work, then you can just Google it...

Special thanks to:

Google.com

Entrepreneur.com

The Market Donut

RayvanBros.com

Junesh Acharya

Julie Holland

Info Entrepreneur, a Canada Business Network

Brian Tracy

Mark Macdonald

Robert Cialdini

Susan Ward

Forbes.com

Nicole Robinson, CEO of Gloss and Glam

Kerwin Steffen

Dumb Little Man.com

Alex Palmiere from Motivation Grid.com

Kathrin Tschiesche from Bookbon.com

Numerounonweb.com

ReliableSoft.com

Jeff Saxton of the Social Media Examiner.com

FYI Print Art

Marty Zwilling from Business Insider.com

Smallbusiness.co.m.chron

MarketingSchools.org

Webanalysis.blogspot.com

Mediapost.com